What to do
when you find out...

YOUR WIFE

WAS

SEXUALLY

ABUSED

*What to do
when you find out...*

YOUR WIFE

WAS

SEXUALLY

ABUSED

JOHN COURTRIGHT
& DR. SID ROGERS

with Discussion Guide

ZondervanPublishingHouse
Grand Rapids, Michigan

A Division of HarperCollinsPublishers

Your Wife Was Sexually Abused
Copyright © 1994 by John Courtright and Sid Rogers

Requests for information should be addressed to:
Zondervan Publishing House
Grand Rapids, Michigan 49530

Library of Congress Cataloging-in-Publication Data

Courtright, John, 1956–
    What to do when you find out—your wife was sexually abused :
    with discussion questions / John Courtright and Sid Rogers.
        p. cm.
    ISBN 0–310–44291–5 (soft)
    1. Spouses of adult child sexual abuse victims. 2. Adult child sexual
    abuse victims—Psychology. I. Rogers, Sid, 1955– . II. Title. III. Title:
    Your wife was sexually abused.
    HV6556.C68 1994
    362.7'64'082–dc20   94–32057
                                                 CIP

The anecdotal illustrations used in this book are composites of real situations
with names and circumstances fictionalized to protect the privacy of the individuals involved.

Edited by Tim McLaughlin
Cover design by Tammy Johnson
Cover photography by J. Jeffers/Superstock

Printed in the United States of America

94 95 96 97 98 99 / ❖ DH / 10 9 8 7 6 5 4 3 2 1

To Jeanne and Nancy,
whose courage and openness have inspired us,
and whose love and devotion give us great joy.

Contents

Acknowledgments

Dr. Jim Cassens deserves many thanks for initially encouraging us to write this book and for providing necessary counsel and support when we most needed it. His wisdom and patience were invaluable.

We are indebted to Dr. Dale Ryan for his enthusiasm and vision. His support of our seminars played an important role in having this book published.

Thanks also go to our Tuesday night "Grace Group" for their consistent prayers, faith, and encouragement.

Thanks to Scott Bolinder for his enthusiasm for the book, to Sandy Vander Zicht for believing in us and for her thoughtful suggestions throughout this process, and to the rest of the Zondervan team for their encouragement and support.

Thanks to the elders of Grace Evangelical Free Church of La Mirada, California: Steve Borja, Larry Brooks, Neil Greer, and Jeff Scattareggia. Their support and encouragement has made it possible for us to minister to the larger Body of Christ.

Special thanks to all the men who freely shared their stories with us. Their input shaped our thoughts and now our words.

Many others deserve special thanks: Dave and Diane Larson for being true friends while we were learning—the hard way—many of the lessons contained herein (and thank you, Dave, for being the second person to suggest that we write this book); our parents, Richard and Evelyn Courtright and Charles and LaDonna Rogers, whose daily prayers and support sustained us throughout the writing of this book; Debbie Brooks for her assistance in creating the graphics; "the boys" at Active Aircraft Welding, Inc. for providing a quiet haven in which to write, laugh, and find encouragement.

Lastly, saying thank you to our Lord seems woefully inadequate, when we are continually amazed by what he has done with the thoughts he gave us in the first place. May he be glorified in this work.

Introduction

In a landmark survey of more than nine hundred women in 1979, Harvard Ph.D. Diana Russell uncovered the following facts:

- Fifty-four percent of the women had experienced some unwanted sexual violation by the age of eighteen.
- Thirty-eight percent had been sexually molested.
- Only two percent of the cases of abuse occurring within the family and six percent of those occurring outside of the family were ever reported.[1]

Although we may not know the extent of the abuse taking place behind closed doors, what we do know prompted one author to write, "If this were a disease . . . we would declare it an epidemic bordering on a national disaster!"[2]

More recent studies, conducted in a day when women feel more freedom to talk openly about the subject, give us a more accurate understanding of the widespread incidence of sexual abuse. The estimated rate of sexual abuse hovers consistently around the twenty-five percent mark—which translates into a staggering twenty-five million adult women in the U.S. who have been sexually abused.[3] It is a vast tragedy that shatters lives, families, and marriages in every community.

Your Wife Was Sexually Abused, however, is not written primarily for the women who themselves have been victims of sexual abuse (though there is much here that can help them to understand what their husbands are experiencing and what interpersonal dynamics are at play in their marriage during this difficult period in their lives). *This book is addressed instead to husbands of women recovering from past sexual abuse—men who are dealing with their wives' struggles to break free from the effects of past sexual abuse.* If you know such a man—or are married to him—this book will be of immense help to him.

Furthermore, the principles in this book apply beyond sexual abuse to most forms of childhood abuse—physical, emotional, and verbal as well as sexual.

We have written this book from our personal experience as well as from the experiences of hundreds of men we have met and talked with about their wives' childhood abuse. This book was written in the trenches by foot soldiers, not by generals in a strategy room far from battle. So if these pages eerily mirror your situation, it's not because we've been peering through your windows or reading your mail. We know what you're going through because we've gone through it, too.

The content of this book was taken from material originally presented as a seminar for men: "Out of the Line of Fire: Helping Men Survive Their Wives' Recovery from Past Sexual Abuse." Some of the military images in that seminar have found their way into these pages; if they are difficult to relate to or unhelpful, try to discard the images without dismissing the content. They have been included only because of their nearly universal appeal to the men we encountered.

The book is divided into three sections:

- Chapters 1 through 5 describe the cataclysmic changes that take place in a marriage when a woman begins her recovery from past sexual abuse.
- Chapters 6 through 9 explain what a man must understand to survive when his wife's crisis becomes his crisis.
- Chapters 10 through 12 offer practical principles for

how a husband can play a significant and positive role in his wife's recovery.

Because the ideas in the book build from one chapter to the next, we recommend you read through the chapters consecutively rather than skipping chapters or jumping to a point in the book that seems applicable to your present circumstances.

Sadly, many marriages have been splintered on the rocks of past sexual abuse. Many children have been raised without one of their parents because ending a painful marriage seemed the only option, considering the complex, aching issues brought into the relationship by a person's abusive past. Many men and women are left in loneliness, pain, and hopelessness because they do not understand the dynamics of a relationship in which at least one of the partners suffered an abusive past.

It is to all of those who suffer the secondary effects of such abuse—and particularly to husbands—that this book is written. If just one marriage can be saved, one family held together, one man encouraged to persevere, one woman helped toward recovery by a husband who knows how to help—then we have accomplished our goal.

Chapter One
When the Past Crashes into the Present

John's Story

A brilliant midwestern autumn had quickly moved into winter. Stately trees were clothed only in bare twigs and branches. The nip in the air made me all the more anxious to hurry inside. On the doorstep I slipped the key into the lock and thought how glad I was to be home.

But as I shut the door behind me, I sensed immediately that something was terribly wrong. Instead of finding the curtains flung open to catch the last rays of the setting sun, they were drawn tight, turning the autumn dusk into night. No lamp was on. The house was black. The joyful greeting of my wife, Jeanne, was strangely absent.

As I put down my briefcase, I noticed the familiar textbooks laying on the coffee table—a sure sign that Jeanne was home and not at the library, still studying for her midterm exams in graduate school. I took off my coat and unwrapped my scarf, then quietly made my way down the hall toward the bedroom. Maybe Jeanne had come down with the latest flu bug making its way around campus.

That something was wrong continued to weigh on me as I entered the room. My fears were confirmed by the sight of Jeanne huddled in bed, completely hidden by blankets, sobbing inconsolably.

I sat on the edge of the bed. "Honey, what's wrong?" I asked as gently as I could.

"I . . . really . . . don't . . . know," she said through tears. And she truly didn't.

During the last several weeks, Jeanne had been sinking deeper and deeper into a depression she couldn't explain. At times she felt nearly overcome by a pervasive emotional numbness. Both Jeanne and I eventually concluded that the stress of her rigorous master's degree program was responsible for the crisis. But the real cause emerged a few months later during one of her therapy sessions (she had begun therapy as part of her graduate program in clinical psychology), when Jeanne told her psychologist, Bill, about her depression. He sensed a deeper issue behind Jeanne's emotional turmoil. Two simple yet insightful questions Bill asked her turned Jeanne's world upside down.

"How old do you feel?"

"Seven or eight years old," she replied, to her surprise.

"What happened to you when you were seven or eight years old?"

Without warning Jeanne's past came crashing into the present as she made the connection between her past sexual abuse and her present depression. For the first time she realized that what seemed to have happened to her in another lifetime was still haunting her every step.

It was time, she realized, to face her past in order to survive her present.

Jeanne would never be the same; neither would I. Though Jeanne had told me about her past sexual abuse during our courtship, she had narrated it so impassionately that I considered it nothing more than a tragic occurrence in the past that had no long-lasting effects.

I couldn't have been more wrong.

Once Jeanne's crisis became my crisis, I was afraid. I wanted to support Jeanne during this time (without knowing how), yet I was reluctant to get too close to her for fear I'd be dragged down—against my will—into her dark depression. I felt out of control. I realized that I had underestimated the power that past sexual abuse could have. And I had underestimated how deep and resistant to healing such wounds are when they are caused by this kind of devastating personal violation. That a victim's pain can remain hidden for years or (more tragically) for a lifetime, I didn't learn until much later.

Sid's Story

Our twelve-year marriage had been characterized by a steady, growing sense of stability and closeness—quite an accomplishment, considering we had moved six times in four years and had survived my seminary training. We finally settled in to pastor a southern California church, and Nancy gave up her teaching career to stay home and nurture our son, Daniel.

As Daniel began exercising his independence, Nancy was surprised to sense rage welling up within her. Hearing her normally easy-going child defiantly say "No!" or interpreting his tears as proof that she was a bad mother pushed buttons of rage inside of Nancy. She even left the room at times for fear of what she might do to him.

Confused by her overreaction to attitudes and behaviors typical of small children, Nancy sought help from a professional counselor. She read as many books about anger as she could find. She diligently prayed without ceasing for God to take these frightening, intense emotions away.

Yet without relief.

One evening Nancy read that "often the lethargic, depressed, and angry person was physically, emotionally, or sexually abused."[1] She had never considered that her anger could be related to an abusive experience from her past. She wondered if she had ever been sexually abused. She read on:

> Sexual abuse refers to any form of sexual contact or conversation in which the child is sexually exploited for the purpose of bringing sexual gratification to the exploiter. This could take the form of exploratory or stimulating contact with the child or requesting and demanding manual or oral stimulation from the child. It could be much less direct. Suggestive or derogatory talk can be very harmful. Even when no physical contact has occurred, the impact can be powerful.[2]

Memories of things that had happened to her as a child came flooding back into her consciousness. She saw faces and rooms—then felt a rush of painful feelings. She went numb and short of breath. What she had suppressed from her conscious memory for years started gushing back to the surface. At her next counseling session she narrated her horrible memories. But how would she bring herself to tell me? How could she broach this difficult subject after years of marriage, when she had never before spoken a word of it to me?

Not long after that we stood together at the kitchen sink, doing the dinner dishes. We had paused for a moment to watch a tree outside the kitchen window sway in the evening breeze. Her heart beating in her ears, Nancy broke the serenity of the moment.

"Sid, I told you that I was sexually abused when I was a child, didn't I?"

A thousand thoughts and questions tried to force themselves into my consciousness as I grappled with the enormity of the bomb Nancy had just dropped. I uttered a single word that was as much a plea as it was a reply: "No."

Memories that had stalked Nancy for years pounced, and

the secret was finally out. Life for Nancy and me had just irrevocably changed.

Whether in the quiet and solitude of a dark room, or faced with an angry woman—millions of men discover they are married to a woman suffering from the effects of past sexual abuse. Husbands such as John mistakenly view this tragic chapter in their wives' pasts as irrelevant to the present. Other husbands, like me, feel robbed of the relative peace and stability of their marriage by an unexpected intruder from the past. In any case, the moment of revelation is the beginning of a crisis the extent of which most husbands cannot comprehend.

Our stories capture the moment we came face to face with this crisis. The remainder of this book describes how we learned to successfully deal with it. Although each husband's experience is unique, men who have struggled through this type of crisis—or who are now struggling through it—can learn important lessons, as much from our failures as from our successes.

We are writing as neither professional psychologists nor armchair theoreticians, but *as men who have been where you are*. The principles in the following chapters can help you know what to do when you discover that your wife was sexually abused—and can demonstrate that there is hope, no matter how dark life seems.

Questions for Thought and Discussion

1. Can you remember any of the details surrounding the moment you first learned that your wife had been sexually abused?

2. What were your first *thoughts* when she told you?

3. What were your first *feelings* when she told you?

4. How did you respond to your wife when you first learned of her abuse?

5. Did you have any idea then of the changes this would bring into your life and marriage?

Chapter Two
Early Warning Signs

At 4:30 A.M. on January 17, 1994, Southern California was rocked by a magnitude 6.8 earthquake that flattened multilevel buildings, severed freeway overpasses, and triggered thousands of aftershocks that continued for six months.

But, scientists continue to warn, it wasn't The Big One.

The Big One, when it comes, may be a hundred times stronger than the Northridge quake. But whether or not that disaster lies a few years or a few decades into the future, no one knows.

Emotionally jolting and distressing events in our personal lives are no easier to predict than seismic events. "Is there a way to predict if I'm going to experience this kind of crisis?" asked a man in the first seminar we held to help men understand and grapple with the issues raised by their wives' past sexual abuse. This husband suspected that something was wrong, but couldn't put his finger on it. Like seismologists interrogated by the media about The Big One, we could say only that, when the pressure builds up enough over time, it *will* happen. As to *when*, no one can tell.

Conversations with hundreds of men who have unexpectedly been hit with "The Big One"—as well as our personal experience with wives who have been sexually abused—have convinced us that, although you may not know *when* the crisis will occur, at least five early-warning signs suggest that your wife's history of sexual abuse will eventually become a serious crisis both for her—and for you.

Early Warning Sign 1: Any certain knowledge you have that your wife has been sexually abused.

If your wife tells you that she was sexually abused in the past, don't let her emotional passivity fool you into thinking that the abuse was merely an unfortunate, isolated episode in her past. The effects of past sexual abuse will likely surface in a woman's life in some way at some time. Like her shadow, it will never leave her alone, no matter how fast or how far she runs.

Early Warning Sign 2: A change in your wife's attitude toward sex.

If your wife's abuse was sexual in nature, it only makes sense that the experience would mar her whole sexual attitude. Yet this sign is often overlooked if a couple's early sexual experiences lack any hint of sexual dysfunction, in spite of past sexual abuse. All seems well until your wife begins to deal with her past abuse, which may not happen until many years later. Then the picture changes. She may be repulsed by sex, afraid of sex, ashamed of her sexuality. She may have problems achieving an orgasm. Such issues can telegraph a coming crisis that is rooted in past sexual abuse.

Early Warning Sign 3: Exceptional sensitivity to the subject of sexual abuse.

Sally made Jim mute the TV when the evening news reported a child-molestation story—or else she left the room. Few people are not horrified by such a crime, but Sally's extreme reaction highlighted the fact that she was more deeply affected than most. Because she had been sexually abused herself and personally knew the pain, terror, and guilt felt by a child being molested, she identified with what that child had to suffer—and couldn't endure the thought of it. All of this occurred prior to Sally's conscious dealing with her past abuse and could have served as an early warning, if Jim had recognized the signs.

Early Warning Sign 4: A significant distrust of others.

When Peter hung up after answering a telephone survey one night, Jane reprimanded him for giving out personal information to a stranger. Peter just shrugged it off. After all, he hadn't volunteered anything particularly personal. The more he thought about it, however, the more he realized how pervasive was Jane's distrust of others. It was even a standing joke between them about how she didn't trust anyone. It wasn't funny later, after they realized that her distrust was a consequence of her past abuse. This pattern of distrust is particularly apparent when the abuse occurs at the hands of a family member. When those closest to you violate your trust and abuse you, you learn to trust no one.

Early Warning Sign 5: A wife's display of highly intense emotions.

While occasional intense emotions are a normal part of everyday life, uncommonly deep depression (that which exceeds the usual emotions associated with stressful changes in one's life, such as Jeanne's in chapter 1) or intense anger (such as Nancy felt when her son defied her) are signs of a deeper issue. A woman's paralyzing fear of being out after dark, or her extremely sympathetic identification with the underdogs in life may be signs that her sexual abuse is indeed affecting her present life. This impact may become much more pronounced when she begins to deal openly with her past abuse.

Although any one of these signs may signal to a husband that his wife has been sexually abused, it's a mistake to believe that knowledge can avert the coming crisis. No preventative measures can sidestep the inevitable. A seismologist's early-warning signs may tell you that The Big One is coming, but they can't tell you when and they can't keep it from happening. Whether you see the signs or not, the odds are that the crisis will come. And when it does, it will shake you to your very core.

A woman who has been sexually abused may show some of these signs, all of them, or none of them. Yet if you notice some of these early-warning signs in your wife, there is a reasonable chance that she experienced some form of abuse in her past. A sure sign of crisis, though, is when her past abuse lurches into the present and turns what may have been relative calm in your home to chaos.

Questions for Thought and Discussion

1. Do you know for certain that your wife was sexually abused?

2. When did your wife inform you that she had been sexually abused?

3. What was her emotional state when she told you?

4. Did you see any of the early-warning signs listed in this chapter? If so, which ones?

5. Can you add any early-warning signs that you observed in your wife, beyond those listed in this chapter?

Chapter Three
Ripples of Chaos in a Life of Calm

Two years ago Sid's family rented a couple of cottages with his brother and his brother's family and enjoyed a week's vacation on a small lake in northern Minnesota. He remembers that his favorite part of the vacation was relaxing in a lawn chair near the shore at the end of a busy, active week. Life doesn't get much better than seeing the varied colors of a sunset sky and watching the choppy lake become smooth as glass as the afternoon wind dies to a mere twilight breeze. I drank in the peacefulness as a parched man drinks water in a desert.

But the serenity of the interlude was brief. The lake no sooner became calm than the thrill seekers arrived, their boats piercing the silence, the skiers churning the surface into rooster tails on their final run of the day. They did an impressive job of turning calm to chaos.

When a woman begins dealing with her past sexual abuse, her calm—and your calm—become chaos. Like a rock thrown into a still lake, the disturbance ripples out in every direction, influencing everyone and everything in its path.

Even after a wife's crisis unfolds, her husband is usually

unaware how profoundly it will affect almost every area of her life and their relationship. Within a brief period of time, powerful changes may forever alter the way she views herself, her relationships, and you.

Changes in the Way She Views Herself

She may become depressed, finally feeling again the hurt of the crime committed against her. She may feel angry that it happened and that she has to deal with it at this point in her life. She may be weighed down by feelings of guilt or dirtiness at having been used by someone in such a vile and disgusting manner. She may desperately replay every memory to determine if she unwittingly did something to cause this horrible thing to happen to her. Thoughts that she somehow *asked* to be sexually abused may torment her. She may punish herself for not having been able to make her abuser stop.

In any case, she will struggle as she processes overwhelming thoughts and feelings and seeks some measure of healing and wholeness.

Meanwhile, you sense the upheaval taking place in her life without fully comprehending the magnitude of the issues she is dealing with inside. You sense her confusion and pain, but at this point the ripples of chaos haven't yet rocked your boat.

It was when she sought professional help that Sid first knew his wife was struggling. *I'm glad she's taking care of herself*, he thought. *I hope the counselor can give her some insight into what's going on and can help her reestablish her equilibrium*.

But he didn't imagine the depth of her pain—nor did he anticipate that the day would come when he would get caught up in the turbulent effects of the past abuse in her life.

Changes in the Way She Relates to Her Family of Origin

The ripples spread from your wife to her relationships with her family of origin. If the abuse came at the hands of her father, grandfather, brother, or uncle, her relationships with her entire family will be dramatically altered. Perhaps she will herself open the secret to her family, despite fears of blowing the family apart by the revelation. She may phone siblings to find out if they also were abused. She may confront the abusing family member (or members) with his crime, risking his denial of what she now knows to be the truth.

Even if her abuser wasn't a family member, she has serious issues to resolve regarding her family. Why didn't her family help her when she needed them most? Why didn't she feel free to talk to any of them about it? If they knew about the abuse, why didn't they do anything about it? Why didn't they believe her or take her seriously if she *did* tell them about it? Why did they leave her so vulnerable?

In short, the ripples of her crisis permanently alter her perception of her family—and it's a painful adjustment for everyone.

You may be confused by your wife's intense feelings toward her family. One day everything seems fine. You take part in the customary family gatherings, phone calls, gift exchanges. Then suddenly your wife distances herself from her family, leaving you standing in the middle, scratching your head.

For all his married life, one man told us, all his wife could say about her childhood family was glowing and wonderful. But the day came when she turned on them with a vengeance. The ruse was up, and she was tenacious in exposing the truth of her family's sins against her. You may feel awkward explaining to her family members your wife's withdrawal from them; or you may feel bad for them when she becomes brutally honest with them.

But on the other hand, you may be as angry with them as she is.

Changes in Her Friendships

Who among her circle of friends can she tell about her past abuse? *What* should she tell them? Can they be trusted with this intimate secret? Will they be sensitive and supportive of her, or will they just make light of her pain and tell her to get on with her life? What will they think of her when they find out what happened? Will the tragic secrets of her past become a burden too heavy for them to bear? Is she asking too much of them to need their support while she rides an emotional roller coaster through the crisis?

Until she arrives at answers to questions like these, she may distance herself from her friends, unsure of where she stands with them. She may want to avoid people with whom she has only casual relationships. Small talk seems like meaningless chatter and no longer appeals to her.

You may feel like she is pulling away from the very people that care about her and that can support her. You may want to say something, but inside you suspect that your words may result in her directing some of her intense emotions toward you.

Changes in Her Walk with God

The ripples from her crisis move upward, too. She may have serious doubts about God's love and power. If God really loves her, why did he allow this to happen to her? If he is so powerful, why didn't he stop this person from hurting her? Serious questions about God may make her actively resist attending church. She wants nothing to do with church—unless she feels that its people are open, honest, and genuinely concerned for her welfare. She despises being asked "How are you doing?" several times each week, especially by people she believes really don't care, but who ask only out of habit.

You feel very uncomfortable during this time, too, particularly if you end up attending church by yourself, or if you are actively involved in church ministries. Responding to "Where is your wife?" for the fiftieth time in one day leaves you frazzled and frustrated. (We offer some help with this practical issue in the section entitled "Commonly Asked Questions and Answers.")

Changes in Her Relationships with You and the Children

Most significantly, the ripples of chaos impact her immediate family. At some point you and your children are affected by the disturbances your wife's past abuse is creating in every dimension of her life. She may become distracted and emotionally distant from her children. Her attention may become fixed on the people and the events that occurred in another place and time. New insights about what she is like and what she wants from others redefine her relationship with her children.

Her relationship with her husband, furthermore, is also carried into this churning chaos. As she focuses on her abusive past in order to recover from it, unexpected and radical changes in your wife make you ask yourself the same question, over and over: What's going on? You most likely will not understand why this is happening or what to do about it.

Daryl certainly didn't. It wasn't long after his wife had started therapy that he joined her for a session. He was just confused, Daryl told the therapist. Although he and Martha used to have fun together, spending their free time with one another and the children, Martha had recently begun drawing into herself, wanting to be alone. She was physically exhausted. She felt like she had nothing to give Daryl or the children. Captivated by the atrocities of her past, she was emotionally numb. The painful memories overwhelmed her and exhausted her reserves. She felt dead—and Daryl sensed the change.

Daryl was willing to give Martha some space, a chance to do what she needed to do—but he still didn't understand what was going on. He didn't understand that Martha was in a state of shock. Her past had hit her like a train coming out of nowhere; she never heard the whistle, and she hadn't had time to get off the tracks. Now seriously crippled, her body, mind, and emotions began to shut down as all her energies were directed toward the process of healing.

Yet the changes in their lives sparked by this crisis unsettled Daryl. "What's going on?" he kept asking. "When will it all end? How can we get life back to normal?"

As your wife uses more of her time and energy to recover from the effects of past sexual abuse, everything in her life *and* yours will be disrupted. Inevitably, *her* crisis becomes *your* crisis.

Questions for Thought and Discussion

1. Describe your life before your wife began her recovery from past sexual abuse.

2. What were the first changes you noticed in your wife once she began her recovery process?

3. How did these changes affect her life?

4. How did these changes eventually affect *your* life?

5. What impact did these changes have on your children or others associated with your wife?

Chapter Four
When Her Crisis Becomes Your Crisis

I t was late one afternoon during his childhood that Sid's family's first color television was delivered. Only a few weeks after the fall line-up of new programs hit the air, the delivery man hauled into the family room a cardboard box with the word ZENITH printed on it in large letters. "It was as if we were watching the birth of a litter of puppies," Sid relates. "My mother, my brother, and I all stared as he carefully cut away the box to reveal a brand-new color television."

The first viewing of a show, however, was painfully delayed until his dad got home from work. And then he made the unpopular executive decision to eat dinner first.

It was seven o'clock before everyone was seated in the family room in their customary positions. Dad then eased himself out of his recliner, strode over to the new Zenith, and with controlled pride turned the power knob on. A brief crackle of static, then . . . the theme song to *Garrison's Guerrillas*, a favorite show. The opening credits rolled over a collage of machine-gun bursts and violent explosions as the program's stars demonstrated their daring. Balls of fire, in vivid orange, exploded before Sid's face. "It was as if I had actually walked onto the battlefield. I could almost feel the heat," he said.

Twenty years later Sid walked onto another battlefield. This one was much more real than even "living color" could portray. "The fact that I hadn't enlisted in this war didn't protect me from devastating explosions when I stumbled through tripwires set long ago by an unseen enemy. Not knowing whether to advance or retreat, I blundered ahead onto ground where, just beneath the surface, mines were primed and waiting. With no basic training to prepare me, all I wanted was a foxhole to protect me from the shrapnel slicing through the air," he recalls.

When the crisis of your wife's recovery from past abuse eventually becomes *your* crisis, you are suddenly caught in the crossfire of a battle you never intended to fight. Where once there was calm, there is now the whistling of incoming mortar shells and the explosions of mines. Everything and everyone in your life is disrupted. Whatever stability you once enjoyed is shattered as nearly everything in your life and in your marriage begins to change.

Your Changing Roles

Your wife's recovery process demands many changes of both of you. As she reexamines her relationships with you and with others, you will find yourself adjusting to shifting roles— at home and elsewhere. This is a difficult challenge. Let's examine these changing roles more closely.

Your changing role at home includes doing jobs once done by your wife.

While Sue was recovering from her past abuse, chronic exhaustion sapped her energy—even when it came to preparing meals for Dan and the kids. So if Dan wanted to eat when he got home, or if he wanted the children to be fed, he had to prepare the meal himself. He also made the kids' lunches and provided transportation to and from school. Washing dishes and general housekeeping were also added to his workday.

Although Dan willingly assumed these chores for a while, he gradually began to resent performing such domestic duties *on top of* his fifty-hour-a-week job. Dan's former pattern of life was being disrupted, and he didn't like it one bit. Not that Sue was relishing the upheaval in her life, either. Both of them were reeling from shifting roles.

Your Changing Sexual Relationship with Your Wife

Jeff couldn't understand how Jill could suddenly no longer be interested in having sex after five years of active, satisfying marital lovemaking.

"How can she go from being an initiator in our sexual relationship," he asked, "to not even wanting to be a participant?"

Jeff's question is answered only by understanding how your wife is affected during her recovery process. An emotionally exhausted woman, numb from processing her feelings related to her past abuse, may have little intimacy to offer her husband. So she simply shuts down physically and emotionally.

Your sexual relationship can be complicated by the sexual nature of her past abuse. As she works through her past, the thought of sex may leave her feeling ambiguous and confused about sex. *How could someone have used her so terribly in this way?* she asks herself. So she questions whether she wants to make herself vulnerable again by engaging in sex.

Meanwhile, you probably don't know where you stand sexually with your wife.

A shift in one's sexual relationship is especially difficult for a man, who typically places immense significance on his sexual relationship with his wife. For sex usually symbolizes his sense of self, his manhood, his potency (particularly in Western society). The process of reestablishing a sexual relationship between a husband and wife when she is recovering from past sexual abuse is delicate, difficult, and filled with pitfalls. Yet the sexual component of the relationship must be addressed to achieve a healthy, thriving marriage.

Your Changing Relationship with Friends

She may no longer have the energy or desire to maintain an active social calendar. During her healing process she may want to spend more time alone, do more things by herself, without you or the family.

Sally withdrew from the very people at church with whom she had had active social relationships. She made it clear that she didn't want to be in any relationship that expected too much of her. She simply felt she couldn't meet such expectations in her present state of turmoil. It seemed better, Sally thought, to keep everyone at arm's distance—rather than get involved with them, eventually let them down, and then feel guilty about not being what they expected her to be as a friend or church member. Because she thought the abuse was somehow her own fault, she didn't need *another* relationship that might contribute to her feelings of guilt. She'd had enough guilt for a lifetime.

But these changes put Jim in an awkward position. "Is Sally all right?" friends would ask him.

"Yes," he answered, although Sally was in tremendous pain.

"Is she sick at home?" they pressed. Jim didn't know what to say. It wasn't as though she had the flu. She was simply distancing herself from all of her relationships. How could he explain this to people without putting both Sally and himself in an even *more* uncomfortable position?

Jim felt more and more isolated and alone himself. The enjoyment he had found in their circle of friends was disrupted by everything that was happening to Sally. He began making excuses to avoid socializing by himself—and this caused him to resent Sally even more.

Your Changing Financial Situation

The expense of your wife regularly seeing a counselor or therapist can be staggering, especially without insurance. With fees around $100 per session (and up), a year's worth of weekly counseling sessions adds up to more than five thousand dollars—an expense that, for many families, means big sacrifices must be made.

In order to free up funds for her therapy, Yolanda and Peter took their children out of private school and stopped their music lessons. Greg and Vicki postponed several financial goals they had set: saving for another car, covering the expenses of a much-needed vacation, putting aside money for their kids' education and their retirement. Both Peter and Greg were committed to their wives' recovery to the extent that they committed their limited financial resources to the process.

Neither these men nor their wives ever dreamed they would face such a decision. The fact is, few families think of adding the expense of therapy to their long-range financial planning. Yet they must make adjustments.

Your Changing Feelings about Your Situation

With everything shifting around you—household operations, your sexual relationship, your friendships, your finances—you may experience intense feelings churning inside of you. At first you may have been pleased that your wife was taking care of herself and getting some help. But now that so much in your life is changing, you aren't so sure. Men who attend our seminar commonly express four feelings at this point: confusion, isolation/abandonment, fear, and anger.

Confusion

A man frequently asks:

- "What's going on here?"
- "Why is my wife acting this way?"

- "Why are things so different now?"
- "When will our lives get back to normal?"

The disruptions to your "normal" way of life, unfortunately, lead straight to confusion. Few events in a man's experience prepare him to understand what has happened, to provide at least a context for his confusion. And seldom does he know what to do next.

Isolation and abandonment

As your wife withdraws from you, from your family, and from your friends, you may feel abandoned—especially if she was the one who supported you during stressful periods and in whom you confided. In short, you feel as though you've lost your best friend:

- She isn't there to talk with anymore; instead she's consumed with what happened to her, consumed with those who abused her, consumed with those who stood by and did nothing to help her.
- She isn't there for you sexually anymore because she's painfully aware of the sexual nature of what happened to her. In fact, just the thought of having sex is repugnant and disturbing to her.
- You may feel she isn't there for you emotionally, because she can't feel a thing; her emotions are numbed by the pain from the past.

Fear

John went through feelings of fear as a result of his wife's crisis. He remembers: "It made me want to run away as fast and as far as I could—if not literally, then in every other way possible. It scared me to death to see her withdrawing from everyone and everything that was safe and familiar in our lives, into a dark and foreboding world. The more she withdrew, the more afraid I became.

"At the time, I described this unfamiliar, sinister feeling as a 'black hole.' The effects of her past abuse felt like a massive force, relentlessly pulling everything and everyone they touched down into a maelstrom of destruction.

"'I don't know where you're going with this thing,' I felt compelled to tell Jeanne, 'but I'm not going there with you.'

"Yet somewhere inside of me lurked the notion that, as a 'good husband,' I was expected to intimately share her experience, though I feared it would undo me. I didn't know how to be supportive of my wife during this early period of crisis. Far from supporting her, I feared to even get *near* her. *I* certainly wasn't going to be sucked into this black hole and destroyed.

"Jeanne and I had always been inseparable. We had done everything together, gone everywhere together. We liked the same food. We listened to the same music. In fact, we shared a single corporate identity that subsumed my individuality. In psychological terms, my personal boundaries were weak.

"What I didn't realize at the time was that Jeanne and I were two separate individuals. Although I felt she was dragging me with her into a black pit, I didn't realize that I could make personal choices apart from Jeanne's choices for herself. It took several months of time and the help of a therapist and friend to detect my faulty thinking. Once I reestablished healthy boundaries for myself, I no longer felt afraid of what Jeanne's recovery process would do to me. Instead I began to see how I could help the situation."

Some men cannot or are unwilling to consciously acknowledge that they are afraid. Yet other men speak freely of their fears during the crisis of their wives' recovery from past sexual abuse. You may fear, as they do, that—

- Your wife will leave you and end your marriage.
- Your children will suffer disastrous consequences as a result of the changes in your wife.
- Your family will be destroyed financially by the heavy cost of your wife's healing.

- Your wife's counseling is making her worse rather than better when she comes home from therapy more depressed and withdrawn than when she left.
- Her male counselor is stealing your wife away from you—or, at the very least, turning her against you.
- Life will never be the same again.

The fears that men face in this situation are numerous, intense, and exacerbate an already-difficult situation.

Anger

You might be angry at your wife. You might be angry at her abuser. You might not know with whom you're angry. If you spoke your thoughts, you might sound like other men we've heard from in this situation:

- "Why should I or my wife have to pay for someone else's sin? The abuser should be punished for it, not me, not her."
- "Why should I have to put in fifty hours a week at the office, only to come home and find that there's more work here to do? It isn't fair!"
- "Why should we spend our hard-earned money on something that's destroying my relationship with my wife? Her counseling sessions seem to be making her more combative than ever."
- "I have a right to enjoy sexual intimacy in our marriage. But it feels like she's holding out on me—and not because of something I've done."
- "I shouldn't be put in the uncomfortable position of making excuses to friends about her absence or her hostility."

Such disruptions leave you unsure of what's happening, where it's all leading, and what you can do to wrest some calm again from the chaos. Add to these feelings depression and stress, and you're in a particularly unsettling predicament. You long for more peaceful days—and finding none may be the most frustrating thing about this time for you.

Most men are anxious to help their wives come through this crisis. Such a husband wants to help his wife recover, wants her to feel happy again. He wants to be happy *himself* again. He'll do nearly anything to return things to normal. And too often he expects calm to replace chaos in much less time than it actually takes.

Joan came over one evening to talk about her recovery and its effects on her husband.

"Bob is a good man," she said, "and I know he wants to be supportive of me during this time in my life." She paused before continuing. "But last Thursday he said something that really hurt me. He asked me, 'When do you think we can move beyond your abusive past and get on with our lives?'"

Most men in Bob's situation have asked themselves, if not their wives, this question. When *will* it be over so we can get on with a degree of normalcy in our lives again? We expect healing to come unreasonably quickly. We too quickly tire of the stress and upheaval brought to us by our wives' crises. We want to return to a happier, more peaceful time. We want lives that are glassy smooth, like the lake before boats and skiers churned it into choppy waves.

That time can't come soon enough for husbands. Unfortunately, the chaos usually gets worse before it gets better.

Questions for Thought and Discussion

1. How has your role at home changed since your wife began her recovery from past abuse?

2. How has your sexual relationship with your wife changed?

3. How have your relationships with friends changed?

4. If your wife is in therapy, how has your financial situation changed?

5. Which of the feelings discussed in this chapter have you personally experienced?

6. Have you talked to your wife about your feelings of confusion, isolation/abandonment, fear, and anger? If not, why not? If so, how did she respond?

Chapter Five
Have I Become the Enemy?

U ndetected by enemy radar, Stealth fighters screamed across the desert floor. Wild Weasels jammed enemy electronics, providing cover for sortie after sortie of fighters and bombers. Battleship-launched cruise missiles streaked across the sky with video-guided, pinpoint accuracy, delivering lethal force to their targets.

It was one of the shortest military conflicts in history— just one hundred days—and we were glued to CNN broadcasts of the Persian Gulf War live from Baghdad.

During one televised briefing we heard the stolid voice of a military spokesman calling for the lights to be dimmed. The film began to roll; in the distance we made out a warehouse. As the counter clicked off the frames, we realized that the missile itself was providing us with this up-close-and-personal view as it blazed ever closer to its target.

"Now watch those front doors," the spokesman said.

Guided by a weapons specialist aboard a Navy vessel hundreds of miles away, the million-dollar rocket crashed straight through the warehouse doors and, in a flash of light, obliterated the building.

The men and women of Desert Storm systematically decimated the military might of the enemy with surgical precision—and before our eyes. Unlike World War II, which required the Allies to pummel a city with hundreds of thousands of pounds of bombs, the Persian Gulf War demonstrated our ability to strategically deliver devastating weapons to precisely targeted locations.

Similarly, the generalized turmoil and disruption caused by a woman's recovery from past sexual abuse often takes a turn and becomes much more focused as the weeks and months progress. Now you inadvertently provoke direct, angry responses from your wife—responses aimed not at her abuser, but at you.

It's then you realize that your wife now believes that *you* are the enemy.

Becoming the Target

Two deer stand upright in a "Far Side" cartoon, chatting with each other in the forest. On one's chest are concentric circles—an obvious bull's-eye to any hunter. His pal remarks sympathetically, "Bummer of a birthmark, Hal."

Yet it's no laughing matter to be the target of your wife's anger and verbal attacks.

He couldn't take it anymore, Brad told me in my office after he had calmed down. "The way my wife talks to me and treats me, you would think that *I* was the one who abused her," he explained in exasperation. "Here I am trying my best to deal with the changes that have been taking place—and now I'm the focus of all her rage. It's not fair. I am not her abuser."

Brad experienced what many of us have felt: the noticeable change that occurs during the course of your wife's recovery. This change happens when her feelings of pain and loss over an event or events that occurred long ago become intense feelings of anger directed at you over seemingly innocuous issues. She moves from having a bad day to blaming you for it. Whatever you do, whatever you say triggers an extreme reaction that feels disproportionate to your comment or behavior. You begin wondering if *you* have a target on your chest.

It is during this time that conflict in your marriage escalates. "You don't care about me," your wife accuses.

"Wait just a minute," you protest. "I know I'm not perfect, but I am trying my best to be supportive."

"You only want things your way."

"That's ridiculous—you've *never* complained about this before!" And on and on it goes, spiraling down into a black hole of harsh words. All the emotions you felt early in the crisis intensify as things heat up between you and your wife.

You're more confused than ever. At first you failed to understand why things were changing so drastically. Now you are bewildered to be treated as an enemy. *I'm no saint*, you tell yourself, *but now everything I do is scrutinized and evaluated— and usually found deficient in my wife's eyes. Okay, maybe I should have told her I was going to be two hours late last night, but that doesn't mean that I don't care about her anymore, does it? Everything I do seems to have global implications. There's no margin for error with her anymore.*

If you felt abandoned by your wife as she drew away from you earlier, now you feel her pushing you away. It's as if she doesn't want to have anything to do with you. And sometimes, understandably, you don't want to have anything to do with her, either. It feels like a no-win situation.

It doesn't stop there, either. The anger you felt before is amplified by your feeling of injustice. "We both know that it wasn't me way back then that took advantage of her and abused her," a man wondered aloud to me. "So why am I the one taking all the flak? Why am I the lucky guy who gets punished for what someone else did?"

Tragically, it is at this point that marriages suffer from repeated destructive interchanges between husbands and wives. The damage can be irreparable, and in many cases the marriage soon disintegrates altogether.

After one of our seminars, a young man with tears in his eyes approached us and said, "I wish I had attended this seminar a year ago. My wife and I were unable to relieve the escalating tensions in our relationship and last month she divorced me." His wife's crisis had become his crisis and they saw no way out—except to end the marriage. Far too many relationships end without either partner realizing there is a way through these times of cataclysmic change.

Couples in this phase feel trapped, like they have exhausted all of their options. The reality, however, is that several critical choices still lie before them.

Questions for Thought and Discussion

1. In what ways does your wife view you as the enemy?

2. Describe what you feel about being considered the enemy by your wife.

3. Can you think of any reasons why she might feel the way she does?

4. Have you considered meeting with a trained counselor or therapist to better understand what's going on in your marriage relationship? If not, why not?

Chapter Six
Finding the Emerald City

Wherever on life's road you find yourself, your choices determine your direction and your ultimate destination. The journey toward your wife's recovery from past abuse presents you with many such choices.

In the film classic *The Wizard of Oz*, Dorothy merrily bounds down the Yellow Brick Road singing a bouncy melody as Toto runs as fast as his stubby little legs will carry him. They're off to see the Wizard, who knows the way home to Kansas. Yet at an unexpected intersection of *several* Yellow Brick Roads, Dorothy must choose the only one that leads to the Emerald City, where the Wizard resides.

"Now which way do we go?" Dorothy ponders.

"That way is a very nice way," counsels the Scarecrow, hanging from a post in a nearby field as he points in one direction. "It's pleasant down that way, too," he muses, pointing in the opposite direction. Finally, he crosses his arms, pointing in both directions at once.

"Of course," he concludes, "people do go in both ways."

Choosing in which way to proceed is troublesome because individuals *do* take every possible path. Yet not all paths take you where you want to go. Some choices, deceptively alluring at first, end up taking you nowhere.

Four options confront a husband facing the escalating struggles of coping with his wife's recovery: he can quit, win, lose, or adapt.

Choosing to Quit

Some days it seems like the least painful option is to throw in the towel and separate, if not divorce. Pay forty dollars, sign a few papers, wait six months, and it's over. Yet it's not as painless as it appears. In *The Divorce Decision* author Gary Richmond writes,

> The general false impression is that a person will have a great chance to be happy if she/he dumps the bum or sends the witch away. Studies have proven that this is just not the case. The truth is that you will introduce a new chain of events into your life. If you had known how painful they would be, you would have stayed with the process of working at your marriage problems longer, maybe even until they were solved. If you divorce, you will open your own private Pandora's Box, and what comes out will come to haunt you in some way for the rest of your life.[1]

Divorce doesn't solve the feelings of loneliness or abandonment; it intensifies them. The financial strain of paying for your wife's counseling is compounded by the divorce, for now you have *two* households to support. Neither does divorce necessarily allow you to mainain relationships with your once-close circle of friends. Two couples may be an intimate foursome—but if one couple divorces, the other couple often doesn't know how to act around the now-single individuals, no matter how close a friendship they may have enjoyed earlier. It's too awkward for them to stay friends with both ex-spouses, so they will usually abandon the friendship with at least one of them.

Add to all this the long-term negative consequences of

divorce to your children, to your spiritual life, and to your own extended family (not to mention your in-laws), and the choice for divorce seems less and less inviting. At the time it looks like a way out, and it is—out of the frying pan and into the fire.

Choosing to Win

While winning is a good option in most of life's situations, winning in this context means imposing your will on your wife for your own benefit. You "put your foot down once and for all" and "take charge of the situation" to make sure things go your way. You dictate how and when things will happen in your relationship—regardless of the consequences.

"If you're the man of the house, you have the right to decide how things are going to be done," insisted a man whose wife was in recovery from past sexual abuse. "If you want your wife to pay the bills, then tell her to do it. If you want her to keep the children quiet, tell her to make them stop shouting." He was convinced that his philosophy was pragmatic, rock-solid, and effective.

Unfortunately, this type of conduct exactly mirrors a primary characteristic of the *original* sexual abuse—a man forcing his will upon a woman for his gratification. And it may not be an easy concept for husbands to grasp—they don't recognize that their behavior is essentially abusive. They're blind to any connection between their actions today and something that happened years, often decades, ago to their wives.

Confusing, ambiguous notions of manhood in Western culture only exacerbate the issue. What does it mean to be "the man of the house"? Is a husband's role primarily that of protector-provider? Is he even *supposed* to put his foot down and take charge? (Such critical questions about the dynamics of marriage during the recovery process are discussed in more depth in chapter 10.)

Choosing to win will not promote marital harmony; it can ultimately devastate your marriage. With all the changes your wife is experiencing—and the resulting chaos in your life—to decide that you are going to get what you want, without considering her situation and her needs, may be choosing divorce. Not that you will necessarily divorce her, but that she may divorce you. Not many women who have suffered past sexual abuse are willing to continue living with this kind of abuse.

Choosing to Lose

Choosing to quit is giving up and seeking relief outside the marriage through a divorce or separation. Choosing to *lose*, on the other hand, is also a giving up, but in this way the husband decides it isn't worth all the trouble to win, so he does whatever his wife wants him to do. Instead of getting *his* way, he decides she will always get *her* way.

A husband says, in effect, "Go ahead—walk all over me. It doesn't matter what I want or what I need. My feelings don't matter. Just tell me what you want me to do, and I'll give you no resistance. It just isn't worth it."

Some men attempt to show support and care for their wives by letting them take charge and making sure they get their own way—at least this way, they figure, they don't get battered by the rage and the verbal abuse their wives may otherwise unload on them.

But for even the most patient and long-suffering husbands, this option wears thin. With the best of motives, Jerry chose to lose in his relationship with his recovering wife. He cared deeply for her; he felt badly that she had been so hurt in the past. Because he didn't want her to ever hurt again, he let her do whatever she wanted. He never confronted her, never made his own thoughts or feelings known. Yet Jerry lost something of himself by trying to please his wife in this way. His interests and pursuits became secondary to hers; his career became subordinate to her healing; his desire to be involved with their children became dependent on her approval; his schedule became less important than hers. They had sex only at her (infrequent) request.

Today, though his wife seems to be doing better, Jerry is miserable. He often contemplates suicide.

Granted, it is a precarious balancing act for a husband to remain sensitive to the needs of his recovering wife while still trying to have his own needs met. Forcing his will on her for his benefit—i.e., choosing to win—is only more abuse to her. Yet by allowing her to force her will upon him—choosing to lose— she is, in essence, abusing him.

What should he do? In the healthiest marriages we have seen, both partners clearly communicate their needs to each other. Each do their best to meet the other's needs. This is no less true for husbands and their wives struggling to recover from the effects of past sexual abuse than for anyone else.

There is something a husband can do that will be supportive of his wife while not choosing to lose. It is establishing firm and reasonable boundaries for himself. Psychologist Henry Cloud defines boundaries this way:

> Boundaries, in a broad sense, are lines or things that mark a limit, bound, or border. In a psychological sense, boundaries are the realization of our own person apart from others. . . . It says what we are and what we are not, what we will choose and what we will not choose, what we will endure and what we will not, what we feel and what we will not feel, what we like and what we do not like, and what we want and what we do not want. Boundaries, in short, define us.[2]

Women who have been abused need to do the same sort of boundary building. The early violation of their physical and emotional boundaries makes it difficult for them to recognize later in life what appropriate boundaries are. They either hold people at too great a distance, or they draw them too near. Both extremes are related to one's sense of personal boundaries. Both extremes can be traced back to boundary destruction caused by their past abuse.

Lack of healthy boundaries unfortunately heightens problems in a marriage. "The problem arises when one trespasses on the other's personhood," explain the authors of *Boundaries*, "when one crosses a line and tries to control the feelings, attitudes, behaviors, choices, and values of the other."[3]

Part of the solution is for the husband to model good boundaries. It's not only appropriate for him to communicate his thoughts, feelings, attitudes, likes, dislikes, desires, abilities, and limitations—it's necessary. Such boundary setting lets his wife know where he stands regarding their relationship. Plus, in the mere act of communicating his feelings to his wife, a husband is internally reinforcing his own boundaries.

In relationships that have grown close over a number of years, it's not easy to determine where one person's boundaries end and the other's begin. Yet a spouse can become skilled at discerning appropriate personal boundaries, and more skilled in distinguishing a reasonable request from an unreasonable demand, or realistic expectations from unrealistic ones. And he is more inclined to own his responsibilities instead of being manipulated by his wife's controlling behavior or by his own manipulation of her.

A wife in recovery from past sexual abuse cannot help but be positively influenced by such a husband. Nothing improves a person's boundaries more than to be around someone whose boundaries are definite. If a husband models healthy boundaries within his marriage, it's that much easier for her to begin establishing good boundaries of her own, whether in relation to her husband or to those outside her marriage.

However, it's not uncommon for a woman in recovery to overcompensate in building personal boundaries. Once she begins to establish legitimate boundaries for herself, she may swing from having weak personal boundaries to erecting rigid, inflexible boundaries. A husband who can firmly and lovingly maintain his own appropriate boundaries during this time serves both himself and his wife.

Sandra had been seeing a clinical psychologist for more than five months and was trying to work through her own recovery from past sexual abuse—and she sounded desperate when she told Carl that she needed to continue in therapy. Yet from Carl's perception, things were worse now than they had been just a couple of months ago. Sandra's hostility toward him seemed to have increased; and when she wasn't fighting with him, she was usually depressed.

It took Carl a while to realize that he couldn't indefinitely bear the weight of a disintegrating relationship without help. He needed to talk to someone before it was too late.

So he approached Sandra with the idea of talking to someone about what was going on—and she went ballistic. "How dare you even consider talking to one of your stupid friends about this?" she fumed. "What happened to me is private. It's none of their business!"

But Carl stood his ground. "You may think that because the abuse happened to you, that you're the only one who should be allowed to talk to someone about it. What *I'm* going through right now and what *I'm* feeling is important too! I'm willing to work with you on who I can talk to, but I need to talk with someone!"

At Sandra's next session, her therapist surprised her (and Carl) by challenging her to take Carl's request seriously.

"You've got to remember that week after week you've got me to listen to you, to hear your thoughts and feelings, someone on your side," her therapist said. "Don't you think it's okay for Carl to want that, too?" After a few days Sandra reluctantly agreed with Carl that he could talk to one of the pastors at their church.

By taking his own needs seriously and by refusing to choose to lose, Carl got the help he needed. Talking with a pastor gave him a much-needed relief valve for his feelings, and it also helped him understand what Sandra was going through and how to better communicate his love and concern for her.

"That was a critical time for both of us," Carl remembered. "I'm sure that my being able to talk to someone was instrumental in keeping Sandra and me together through that difficult time."

Sandra discovered some important things through that process, too. "It was terribly hard for me to let Carl talk to someone," she said. "But I came to realize that there were people in my life who could be trusted. That was an important thing for me to learn again during my recovery."

Contrary to first appearances, choosing to lose is not in your wife's best interests. It actually hampers her attempts to build healthy personal boundaries, and it cripples you with anger, resentment, hurt, and loneliness.

Choosing to Adapt

Quitting, winning, and losing, while initially appearing as viable choices, lead only to greater hurt. The future seems bleak when the alternatives are merely these:

- Start over in another relationship.
- Face the loneliness of being single again.
- Try to force your wife to submit to your desires.
- Allow her to force you to submit to hers.

Yet there is another choice: adapting. That is, deliberately crafting a new relationship between yourself and your wife that involves new roles, better communication, and more active caring for each other.

The authors discovered that by choosing to adapt to our unfamiliar and often frightening situations, we began forging relationships with our wives that exceeded our expectations. True, the process of discovery was difficult, spread as it was over years, and colored often by heartache. But the result is stronger, deeper, more satisfying relationships with our wives.

"Does it ever get any better?" men often ask us in despair. It *can* feel like the suffering of both husband and wife will never end. Can our marriage ever get on track again? Can we move forward from here? Can things ever be made right? Will they get better?

For most couples, the answer is yes. The dilemma, however, is that over long periods of time, most couples have cultivated damaging patterns of interaction with each other—obstacles that seem insurmountable, mountains that all but obscure the hope of a renewed marriage. Yet by choosing to adapt to the situation, a husband can begin a new journey with his wife down a path that ultimately leads to a satisfying, fulfilling relationship.

But how will this all come about, husbands want to know. What will this new relationship with my wife look like? How will my choosing to adapt make things better?

Here are some of the specifics that usually result from adapting to your wife as she recovers from past sexual abuse:

She gradually regains the freedom to cultivate intimate relationships.

Rather than pushing everyone—including you—away from her out of fear of being hurt, she may gradually begin drawing closer again to others. Chances are, you will find the lost intimacy of your marriage only if you choose to adapt. Your adapting to her makes it possible for her to freely choose you all over again.

She gradually learns new ways to communicate with you.

Exploring the pain of her past demands that she evaluate herself and her relationships more closely—and to communicate more effectively what she thinks and how she feels. Such communication skills add richness to a marriage.

She finds a new freedom to enjoy and express her sexuality.

Freed from the baggage of the past, from the fear of being abused again, she responds willingly—and may even initiate lovemaking with you.

She acquires a healthy independence.

As she works through the issues of her abuse, she develops an increasing sense of personal worth. She discovers the truth that she is not the bad person she thought she was all those years—and that realization frees her to fully explore the opportunities life offers her.

And her fulfillment spells dividends for your relationship. You will be living with someone who feels better about herself and what she is doing with her life. Instead of dreading to be with an angry or depressed woman, you will look forward to being with a woman who enjoys more of life than she ever did before.

All we hope for in our marriages may be possible, but the hurdle of her recovery from past abuse must be first surmounted—and the only way to surmount it is to adapt. Any other choice invariably causes the marriage to at least falter, and perhaps fall flat on its face.

On the other hand, remember that you're not the only one with choices to make. Your wife has exactly the same set of choices from which to choose: she can choose to quit, win, lose, or adapt. It is as desirable for both spouses to choose to adapt as it is unfortunate for only one to make the choice to adapt. Such disparity of choice gradually but inevitably distances spouses—and frequently leads to divorce.

Although a husband cannot assume responsibility for his wife's choices, he can choose the path *he* will follow. We have seen it happen often: a man chooses to adapt and begins taking the steps we discuss later in this book . . . his wife slowly begins to believe that maybe there is hope for their marriage after all . . .

and this is what often prompts her to make her own choice to adapt.

If you choose to adapt, then the remainder of this book is for you. We can't promise that you'll find the Emerald City of dreams come true, but we can show you a process that has worked for us and for other men like you. The road is difficult, but at least you are on a road that gets you where you want to be.

A word about choosing *not* to adapt: that choice is a choice for more pain, more agony, more of the constant turmoil that you're probably feeling right now. Choosing not to adapt means you'll probably stumble from crisis to crisis, taking one blow after the other until one or both of you reach your limit and leave the relationship.

So consider your choice carefully. If you do choose to adapt, the first step in that direction may surprise you.

Questions for Thought and Discussion

1. What to you are the pros and cons of choosing to quit?

2. In what ways in your marriage have you made a choice to win?

3. In what ways in your marriage have you made a choice to lose?

4. What have been the results of your choices to win or lose?

5. Do you believe that choosing to adapt will result in your finding the kind of relationship with your wife that you've always desired? If so, why? If not, why not?

Chapter Seven
A Friend for All Seasons

Late one evening Father Thomas Fleming was reading a book in his study when the phone rang. Noting the lateness of the hour, the priest expected tragedy. He picked up the phone to hear the voice of a distraught female in his small parish.

"Father Tom, can you come to the hospital?" she pleaded. "I need you here right now. Something's happened to Perry."

He found Connie outside the E.R. entrance, sitting on a cement bench in the stark light of a halogen lamp above her. Only when he was near her did he realize she was weeping. He sat down next to her on the hard bench.

"Perry tried to kill himself tonight," she finally said when she could speak.

Perry had apparently purchased several bottles of sleeping pills at a drugstore, downed a couple handfuls in the parking lot, and drove away—hoping that when the pills took effect, he would roll the car and kill himself. Eventually, as the pills took effect, Perry became afraid and sought help.

The next morning Perry had been assigned a bed in the psychiatric ward, and Father Tom went to visit him.

Embarrassed and still hurting, Perry let Father Tom gently probe to discover why he had tried to take his life.

Finally, painfully, Perry told him. Connie had been going to counseling for a long time in an attempt to recover from prolonged sexual abuse that had occurred during early childhood. She had become distant, uninvolved, self-absorbed, uncaring toward him, Perry said, and it was unfair that he had to pay for the crimes committed by someone else long ago. He hadn't known what to do with the fury he felt toward Connie for the changes she had brought into their marriage and for her unresponsiveness to him. The ongoing upheaval finally drove Perry to seek permanent relief from his pain.

Father Tom left Perry that day, aching for him. The two of them had been friends for nearly a decade, yet in typical male fashion never once did Perry tell him about this struggle—despite the fact that Perry knew the priest could help him, both as a friend and as a minister.

"To be strong a man must be able to stand utterly alone, able to meet and deal with life relying solely upon his own inner resources."[1] This is the generally accepted view of what it means to be male, summed up by Watergate conspirator G. Gordon Liddy. To the contrary, we suggest that one of the best things a husband can do to help his wife during her recovery from past abuse is to *get himself a friend*.

Few deeply ingrained values have gotten men into more trouble than the one that asserts that manhood is measured by a detached, reserved, aloof self-reliance. Yet if we stand alone, we will most likely fall alone. We have forgotten the biblical proverb: "Two are better than one, because they have a good return for their work: If one falls down, his friend can help him up. But pity the man who falls and has no one to help him up!" (Eccl. 4:9–10).

"But I have friends," you protest. Ask yourself: are they friends, or are they buddies? Most men have a number of buddies—the baseball team, the racquetball partners, the church committee members. Buddies fulfill some needs among men, but without *friends* a man may feel truly alone. How many buddies can you tell about the impact your wife's past abuse has on your marriage? How many buddies know that you're so angry you could punch someone? To how many buddies have you entrusted your anguish about feeling utterly rejected by your wife?

With buddies we talk about last weekend's football game and the new deck we put in. Only with friends do we share our deepest dreams and most severe struggles.

We've observed that a man with a friend who walks with him through the tough days of his wife's recovery from past abuse is the man most likely to survive the ordeal. The man with a friend is also likely to contribute to his wife's recovery, not hinder it.

A man has a built-in need for companionship. "It is not good for the man to be alone" was God's evaluation of his creation. Yet when your chosen partner, your wife, is largely unavailable as a friend—or even feels you are her enemy—when your companion consistently questions your motives or attacks you verbally, then you must look for friendship in another person.

Your need for a companion doesn't decrease during crisis, it increases. And because your wife cannot partner with you like she has in the past, you must find friendship with another man. (It doesn't take a rocket scientist to realize that this is not the time to find a friend in another woman.)

Yet men don't readily seek out true friends and foster deep friendships. Why do we have such a hard time nurturing friendships that will help us when we need them most?

A False Sense of Omnipotence

This sense deceives men into thinking they can handle everything themselves, whatever life throws their way. When your wife's crisis becomes your crisis, you feel sure that, without any help, you can hold up under verbal assaults. You can take the rejection without flinching, cook the meals, care for the children, and add other domestic tasks to our already crowded lives. Whatever your wife throws at you, you're convinced you can take it like a man—even the fallout of her past abuse.

And perhaps you can—for a while. Before long, however, your resources run dry in the heat of increased personal, emotional, and financial demands that press you during your wife's recovery process. When you find you're without support in a never-ending firestorm, your sense of omnipotence evaporates. You discover that you do need a friend, after all.

Not Wanting to Appear Needy

Your pride interferes with your wisdom when, in spite of knowing you need a friend, you still don't get one because you don't want to appear needy. The last thing a man wants in a crisis is to appear needy. We're repulsed by our neediness. We hate to be vulnerable. We can't stand feeling like a failure in anything.

Neither do we relish the thought of letting someone know we're hurting. Most of us, in fact, follow the Commandments for Men:

- You shall not cry.
- You shall not display weakness.
- You shall not need affection, gentleness, or warmth.
- You shall comfort, but not desire comforting.
- You shall be needed, but not need.
- You shall touch, but not be touched.
- You shall be steel, not flesh.
- You shall be inviolate in your manhood.
- You shall stand alone.[2]

Keeping up a strong, manly appearance means that we never let anyone behind the veneer to see our needs or our pain. If we let people know we're being hurt by our wives, they'd think we were wimps. Women don't hurt men—at least that's how the story is *supposed* to go.

But you *are* hurt by your wife as she goes through her

recovery from past abuse. When you feel misunderstood and rejected, you need a friend to help you keep things in perspective and to pick you up when you fall.

Not Wanting to Be a Burden

"A man should carry his own weight," we're told. And because we feel the heaviness of the weight we're carrying, none of us is quick to shift that burden onto someone we call a friend. So we rationalize our reluctance to find a friend. *I can't call Jim and tell him about this*, you think. Why not? *Well, he's so busy with work and family responsibilities, not to mention the new position he just accepted at church. The last thing he needs is another breakfast meeting to listen to my troubles.*

And so we continue in our self-imposed prison of pain without getting the help we need, or even giving anyone the chance to help.

Face it—we all need help from time to time. You may need help today, but tomorrow someone else may need *your* help. It's simply part of the routine give-and-take of relationships.

We also must stop protecting others from the weight of our burdens. You can't assume this or that friend wouldn't gladly assume your burden if he knew you needed his help. Friends somehow make time for friends, in spite of hectic schedules. Love enables us to do many things that at first glance seem impossible.

The bottom line is this: ask your friends for help when you need it—then let *them* tell you if they're too busy. Give them the freedom to define their own limits of what they can and can't do to help you.

For example, Sid has a friend named Craig who calls him whenever he feels the need to get together to talk about the struggles in his marriage, and Sid has the freedom to tell him if or when he is available. Craig understands that Sid has other responsibilities, and he doesn't feel rejected if Sid puts him off until next week. It's a healthy relationship: Craig gets the help he needs without feeling like he's overburdening Sid with his problems, and Sid feels the freedom to do what he can.

Afraid of Rejection

The authors are convinced that deep inside most men is a terrible fear of rejection that drives our compulsion to appear as though we never need anything from anyone. We are afraid of our own weakness; even more, we are afraid that if anyone saw our weakness, they would reject us. We are afraid that if we let anyone know we are hurting, that person would gain the upper hand in our relationship with him. We would consequently lose whatever stature we presently have in the relationship.

When Sid started meeting with John, he was afraid of rejection. After all, Sid was the pastor—the one with all the answers, the master helper. Yet there he was, needing help himself. But he took the risk and found that rather than rejecting him, John was actually drawn to him because he had earlier walked the same road. John could sympathize with him. He knew how Sid felt. This common experience bonded them rather than distanced them from each other.

Other men, of course, may have pushed Sid away or minimized his pain or in some other way rejected him if he had shared his burden with them. Which is why you must choose carefully with whom to share your situation.

The two kinds of friends to find are *supportive* friends and *skilled* friends. Supportive friends will "be there" for you—will listen to you and accept you, regardless if they actually understand what you're dealing with. Skilled friends, on the other hand, understand because they've been there. They know what you're thinking, they know intimately your intense and tormenting feelings because they've walked in your shoes, they've asked the same questions. And they just might have reached some conclusions that may prove invaluable to you.

So determine who are your *supportive* friends. Let them

know what's going on so that they can offer their support. Then also connect with a *skilled* friend. There is no help like the help offered by those who have traveled the road before you. They know the curves, the potholes, the blind intersections. Listen to them and let them help you map out a path for yourself.

It was during their early breakfasts that John offered Sid what may have been his best advice.

"Sid, don't try to figure it all out," John said. "Sometimes you just need to keep putting one foot in front of the other."

It was hardly profound counsel, but at that moment it was priceless wisdom. It meant it was okay to feel what Sid was feeling. It was okay to be thinking what he thought and to be asking the questions he asked. It meant that maybe he might never get the answers he wanted—but if he just followed the stretch of the road he could see in front of him (an awful short stretch in those days), things would probably turn out all right.

A man's skilled friend in some cases is a professional counselor or therapist, who—though he may never have personally lived with a wife who has been sexually abused—has walked closely with many men who have. By virtue of their professional training and experience, counselors know the salient issues and can usually provide tremendous assistance along the way.

During the course of conducting several seminars on this topic, not one man has told us we don't know what we're talking about—not even politely. Instead we invariably hear some version of this: "You're right. I do need a friend. Now how do I find one?"

How to Find a Friend

Be discreet.

Don't volunteer the details of your need for a friend at a church prayer meeting or dinner party: "Most of you don't know this, but my wife was sexually abused as a child, and we're having a terrible time of it. I need someone to help me."

For the sake of your wife's privacy, be discreet in your search for supportive and skilled friends. It's difficult enough for her to handle her feelings without having you broadcast her personal information. And going public with such information, even for the good reason of finding a friend, tends to attract people who are interested only in hearing gory details.

Consult with local clergy.

Your pastor or a local support group in your community can guide you to men who can be either supportive or skilled friends. Take advantage of such networking with men who can probably offer the help you so desperately need.

Consider personal counseling.

Many men view counseling as a last resort for those with insurmountable problems—and even then, most men refuse to go. Yet counseling is not the last refuge of the weak. Don't underestimate the seriousness of the issues you are contending with. A professional counselor or therapist can be an invaluable resource to turn to in the situation you face. Take sessions with a therapist either individually or in the form of a support group for the husbands of survivors of past abuse; in either case, counselors can help you cope with the resulting chaos when your wife's crisis suddenly becomes yours.

As we said at the beginning of this chapter, the best way to help your wife is to do something to help yourself by getting a friend. By gathering a few key friends around you to give you support and guidance, you will create an environment within which you can begin to move past your own pain and begin to understand what's happening to your wife. Understanding her recovery process inevitably answers your angry questions about why you always seem to be in her line of fire. More importantly, debriefing with a skilled friend can help you know what constructive action to take to improve your situation and to change your role from enemy to ally.

Questions for Thought and Discussion

1. Of the reasons listed for why men don't have friends (false sense of omnipotence, not wanting to appear needy or be burdensome, afraid of rejection), which one is most applicable to you?

2. Who in your life right now is a *supportive* friend? Who is a *skilled* friend?

3. Have you had success in finding a friend in any of the ways listed?

4. Can you add any more avenues to getting a friend than those already listed in this chapter?

Chapter Eight
Understanding the Recovery Process

I f you want to help your wife during her recovery from past abuse, you must first understand the recovery process. Armed with this knowledge, you will be able to understand what's happening to your wife now and have a better sense of what to expect in the future as she goes through this process.

You must recognize that her recovery from past abuse is a *process*, not a *decision* made at a point in time. Unfortunately, based on what they often tell their wives, men generally believe that recovery should be as simple as waking up one morning and deciding to no longer allow her past to influence her present. Not that women in recovery wouldn't prefer that healing could be this simple. But it's not. Healing of all types, including that of wounds inflicted by past abuse, always takes time.

So the question "When will she get over this?" always receives the same answer: Not until she works through the *entire process of recovery*—a process that is abbreviated only at the risk of incomplete healing.

Some women work through the process faster than others, of course. The pace of recovery usually depends on the severity and duration of the past abuse and a woman's courage or capacity for facing the ugliness of her past. For most women, however, once recovery begins, there's no turning back. The best thing a husband can do is understand the process so he can support it rather than subvert it.

The stages of the recovery process of recovery can be diagrammed:[1]

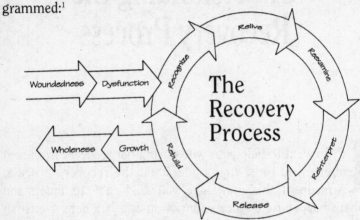

Moving from woundedness to wholeness, a person in recovery passes through a number of stages over a period of time. As you can see in the diagram, the stages of woundedness and dysfunction are prior to the six distinct yet interrelated stages of the actual recovery process: recognize, relive, reexamine, reinterpret, release, and rebuild. The stages of growth and wholeness, finally, are the conclusion to a successful recovery process.

We will consider what takes place at each stage, focusing on those insights that have proven valuable to men whose wives have gone through the process of recovery.

Woundedness

You need first of all to consider the type of wound your wife carries. *Superficial* wounds are those typically remedied with soap, water, and a Band-Aid. *Serious* wounds require special care and time to heal properly—yet such wounds may be so debilitating that even expert care administered over a long period of time fails to completely restore a person to health.

Superficial wounds may hurt like crazy, but they are easily cared for. As a youngster John dreamed up an effortless way to walk—or rather run—his dog, Frisky: tie his leash to his bicycle handlebars, and peddle away. When Frisky lurched after a canine adversary one day, he somersaulted off the bike and hit the pavement—and scraped every exposed piece of flesh against the unforgiving asphalt. His shirt was in ribbons, his back a bloody collage of scratches, scrapes, and burns.

Bike, dog, and boy eventually made it home where he made his planned entrance with flair. "I had a little accident," he announced, exposing his bloody back. His sister screamed, his mother dropped what she was doing and rushed to his side with concern on her face. The effect was gratifying. His mother was standing before the open medicine cabinet, where she discovered there was no Bactine, no first-aid spray, no hydrogen peroxide—only a half-empty bottle of rubbing alcohol. It would have to do.

John is sure his scream was heard for miles. He recovered from his superficial wounds, however, and forgave his mother for her momentary lapse of judgment.

Sid's brother, on the other hand, suffered a serious wound. A jet ski accident left him with a painful knee injury. Figuring he had just twisted it, he stayed off it for the next few days. Yet the pain only increased, and no amount of ice or heat slowed the continual swelling behind his knee.

When the pain became unbearable, he went to the doctor, who at a glance diagnosed an infection. Too serious to treat with oral antibiotics, the infection required surgery: opening the knee in order to clean out the wound.

The wounds our wives have experienced are hardly the superficial, easy-to-care-for variety. Instead they require extensive healing efforts. If husbands could somehow *see* their wives' open, raw wounds caused by past sexual abuse, we might comprehend how much time healing takes. No quick fixes can patch the damage. Time, energy, and skill are needed to bring healing and eventual wholeness.

A husband who understands the serious nature of the wounds his wife suffers also understands that her healing won't be obtained overnight. If the infection of sexual abuse has been festering for twenty years, a great deal of work needs to be done to ensure that every bit of the infection is eradicated. To be sure, significant healing occurs early in the process—but wholeness calls for long-term, patient understanding during each stage.

Dysfunction

A woman's past sexual abuse often triggers patterns of thinking in her that eventually lead to dysfunctional behavior (the prefix *dys-* literally means *impaired*—thus *impaired functions*). Both the thinking patterns and the dysfunction may be defense mechanisms she created to protect herself from being hurt again; or they may be responses to those defense mechanisms.

In *Healing Emotional Wounds*, psychologist Dr. David Benner discusses three defense mechanisms that block the healing of past emotional wounds.[2]

- *Denial.* People who tend to consciously or subconsciously disbelieve the truth about a particular event live, we say, in denial. They pretend that what in reality happened to them never took place.

  The singer of a popular country song bemoans the fact that her man is running around on her. She is suspicious of his reasons for getting home late and the unexplained telephone calls. But she does her best to rationalize away the telltale signs of his unfaithfulness: "Just call me Cleopatra," she laments, "because I am the Queen of De-nial."

Some women who have been sexually abused deny that the event ever occurred. My wife would never have termed what happened to her "abuse" if a definition of sexual abuse hadn't shaken her out of denial into the terrible realization that she had truly been a victim of such atrocities.

- *Repression.* What we can't deny, we repress. Repression is the unconscious exclusion—or repressing—of painful thoughts or feelings from the conscious mind. Our wives may not be able to *deny* that they were abused, but they can *repress* some of the memories or feelings associated with it.

That's why early in their relationship Jeanne could speak to John about her past sexual abuse with such little emotion. It wasn't that Jeanne's wounds from the abuse were healed, but that she was repressing her emotions regarding it. Because many women are successful at repressing painful memories of past abuse, their husbands are completely surprised when the effects of their wives' past abuse come crashing into the present. Contrary to a husband's perception, such issues are not safely confined to the past. As long as a woman is repressing her past, her healing and recovery are impaired.

- *Rationalization.* "Rationalizations," says Benner, "are excuses and explanations that superficially seem plausible but which actually distort or misrepresent reality."[3] The woman who rationalizes often downplays the severity of her past abuse ("It wasn't so bad . . . I know many women who were abused worse than me"). Some women rationalize by believing that they somehow invited unwanted sexual encounters. Or a woman may imagine that the wound was inflicted on her because she was a bad person.

Regardless of the mechanism a woman uses to cope with the woundedness—and regardless of whether the mechanism is the *result of* or *defense against* the pain of her experience—the mechanism can lead to dysfunctional patterns in her thinking and in her behavior. If and when she seeks help in dealing with her past, the connection between her past abuse and her dysfunctional patterns will surface. And when she makes that connection, she moves into the first stage of the actual recovery process.

Recognize

Many women are surprised to learn that their present problems are rooted in their childhood. Nancy, for example, doubted that her anger had anything to do with the abuse that happened so long ago. But when she began to understand the connection between her past and her present, she moved into a place where healing could actually begin, where she could overcome the crippling impact of her dysfunctional patterns of thinking and behaving.

It is usually a traumatic moment when recognition occurs—when a woman's past crashes into the present. So it's understandable that she may want to retreat from the truth of what happened. Yet with encouragement she may walk into an abyss of terrifying memories and gut-wrenching emotions.

If she knows you are committed to walking beside her during this difficult time, it makes her journey a little easier. A husband's unfortunate words ("How could what happened thirty years ago have anything to do with what's happening to you now?") or actions may only confirm a woman's doubts that her past could so powerfully influence her present life. Such words or behavior by a husband hinder his wife's recovery. He does better to encourage his wife to explore the connection between her dysfunctional patterns and the current crisis, often with the help of a skilled professional counselor.

Even when your wife recognizes the connection between events in her past and her present feelings, life—both hers and yours—will get worse before it gets better.

Relive

Life gets worse because her next stage of recovery is typically a reliving of her painful experiences—which inflicts a unique torture on her. Her refusal to deny or repress the past any longer may open a floodgate of painful emotions and memories. From having repressed every 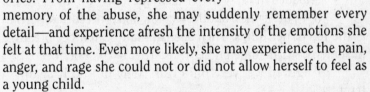 memory of the abuse, she may suddenly remember every detail—and experience afresh the intensity of the emotions she felt at that time. Even more likely, she may experience the pain, anger, and rage she could not or did not allow herself to feel as a young child.

And as you have probably guessed by now, you are also affected as your wife experiences this torture.

"I think my wife's counseling is worthless," men commonly tell us at this stage. "She's getting worse instead of better." We remind them that, yes, it *does* get worse—much worse—before it gets better. But the appalling task of reliving the most painful memories of her abusive past is critically necessary for her recovery.

Do not attempt to comfort your wife with short-sighted comments like "Why continue with your counseling if it makes you feel so terrible? For your own sake, just stop going." Your wife needs tremendous courage to face her past abuse; the last thing she needs is someone to tempt her to escape her pain. Escaping is probably what she has done ever since she was wounded. She needs a husband who helps her face pain, not run away from it.

Different couples have different approaches to helping the wife work through her pain. Whatever approach works usually requires some creativity. Consider this memory of John's: "After an evening out together, Jeanne and I were driving home on a deserted highway as our conversation drifted from the day's events to (again) the abusive events of her past. 'When I think about what has happened to me and how it has affected my entire life,' she said, 'it just makes me want to scream.'

"'Go ahead,' I said.

"She gave me a double take.

"'Why not?' I pressed.

"Jeanne rolled down her window, then looked over at me with an expression that asked, *Are you sure this is okay with you?*

"I nodded in reply to her tacit question. 'Go for it,' I said.

"She put her face out the window and proceeded to scream at the top of her lungs. Then she paused to catch her breath, a mischievous half-smile on her face. 'That felt wonderful!'

"I figured we were on a roll. 'Why not do it again?' I tempted.

"I can only imagine how the scene appeared to an onlooker. A car races down a dark highway, the driver looking straight ahead, a pensive look on his face, while an attractive blonde screams out of the passenger-side window.

"Yet what happened during those brief but amusing moments revealed to me what I could do to help Jeanne. My whimsical suggestion demonstrated to her my support in a tangible way during a difficult time in her recovery. It confirmed to her that I was committed to helping her find creative, constructive ways to express her frustration and anger. It was a small thing for me to do, yet it reinforced my role as an ally in her healing infinitely more than if I had merely told Jeanne that I was on her side and that I would support her."

Such creativity can help husbands demonstrate their caring and support for their wives just when they need it most.

Ironically, a wife's reliving of her past abuse—a critical stage of her healing—is often particularly difficult for her husband. Often he is less interested in his wife's healing at this time than in the speedy return to normal of both of their lives. Between the emotional ups and downs of living with a woman who has been abused and the continual juggling of schedules to cover for her needs—all without a supportive friend, chances are—a man may selfishly desire to end his own pain. Granted, on the surface it looks like this: if only his wife would simply stop dredging up the past, then things would quickly return to normal for both of them.

Yet genuine peace and healing cannot skirt the necessary step of her reliving her pain. If you leave behind a piece of the pain, like a cancer it will spread. As long as you're in for surgery, you might as well get it all out.

Admittedly, it's difficult for husbands to trust in a process they probably never experienced firsthand and to place their confidence in the skill of a professionally trained counselor or therapist they don't know. Ultimately, they must trust the healing of their wife to God—despite the fact that we generally hate it when we're not in control. But take it from two men who have felt your pain, frustration, and despair: the process is necessary and the result is worth it in the end. The darkness lasts only for a season. The light *will* break through.

Reexamine

During this stage—still riding her emotional roller coaster—your wife begins thinking about and deeply considering the facts of what happened in her past. At the time the abuse occurred, she was a child, and only with a child's mind could she understand what was happening to her.

Healing now calls her to view her past abuse through an adult mind. The set of facts she now perceives as an adult may be far different than the set she had earlier imagined. These painful memories, often suppressed, may be difficult to reconstruct for a woman by herself, especially since many abusers insist that nothing actually happened, that the entire story exists only in the imagination of the victim. This process can be extremely disconcerting and potentially devastating to a woman as she grapples for the truth in an attempt to reconstruct the painful memories of her past. But for her to be set free from the past, the truth of what happened must be uncovered at last. "The truth will set you free," Jesus promised (John 8:32).[4]

Reinterpret

Armed with the truth about what actually happened during the abuse, a woman in recovery can begin to reinterpret those events of her past from an adult perspective. She can place the blame and responsibility for the abuse at the feet of those who deserve it, instead of blaming herself and feeling guilty about her own imagined culpability in the situation. She can reinterpret the messages that the abuser directly or indirectly communicated to her. She can sort out the lies from the truth.

One abuser, for instance, continually communicated to his victim that he was doing only what she wanted him to do—and she gradually came to agree with him, at the time of the abuse. But years later, when she looked back at the situation through her adult grid, she saw the lie and began to feel rage at being lied to and manipulated by an adult whom she had trusted.

More often than not, women who have been abused feel guilty about what happened. Reinterpreting the past, then, is the task of shifting their feelings of guilt off themselves and onto the responsible person or persons. Instead of feeling guilt, women need to grieve the loss of trust in a significant relationship.

An abuser commonly tells his victim that if she divulges her experience to anyone else, something bad will happen either to her or to someone she loves. Finally recognizing the extent of manipulation she was subjected to can bring an immense measure of freedom to your wife—and consequently to you. Just as her pain causes her to focus her rage on you, her adult interpretation of her past abuse redirects her guilt away from you and onto the responsible person.

Release

Once your wife has allowed herself to express her pain and loss, she can begin releasing her anger, bitterness, sadness, resentment, and betrayal. "Releasing the anger means giving it up," writes Benner. "It means letting go of my right to revenge. It is forgiving other people for what they did to me."[5] This difficult, complex process requires time, courage, and patience. A woman has made it through this stage of her recovery when she can recount the *events* of her past abuse without experiencing the full force of the *emotions* associated with it. This kind of distancing is neither denial nor repression, but evidence of courageous healing from a past emotional wound.

Both of our wives have reached the point in their recovery where they can tell people about their abuse without feeling the crippling emotions that were once associated with their past. "I was abused," they can now say, "but I'm no longer held captive by the event. I've worked through it. I've seen the lies and I've placed the blame where it belongs. I've unburdened myself of anger and false guilt."

Neil Anderson, author of *The Bondage Breaker* and a former professor of Sid's, used to say that you've forgiven people when you no longer want to exact revenge on them, but instead see them as persons in need of healing themselves. Our wives must take that step of forgiveness if they want to fully heal.

Remember that your wife is generating not a forgive-and-forget pardon to her abuser, a pretending that the ugly event never occurred. It is instead acknowledging the abuse while not letting it master her.

Neither does forgiveness demand confrontation. Some husbands desire to seek retribution on their wives' behalf and many encourage them to confront the abusers to set the record straight. Confrontation is not always a wise or advisable course of action. Sometimes it's not even possible.

The idea of confrontation is controversial among experts and difficult for survivors of past sexual abuse. *The primary consideration in determining the wisdom of confrontation must always be the growth and health of the person in recovery.* A woman wondering whether to confront her abuser or abusers must ask herself some difficult questions:

- What do I hope to gain by confronting my abuser?
- Do I want an opportunity to vent my rage over the way I have been mistreated?
- Is my confrontation a means to assign blame to the person responsible?
- Is the confrontation my personal declaration of independence from the bondage and control of this person in my life?

- Does confrontation signify my proactive choice to be free from the lies and other negative influences of my past abuse?

Although these are legitimate reasons to confront an abuser, a wife must also consider the risks of confrontation:

- What if I confront my abuser only to have the person emphatically deny that the abuse ever occurred?
- What if the abuser admits to a particular action or event, but completely misrepresents the circumstances surrounding it?
- What if the abuser minimizes the significance of the abuse, or becomes hostile for being confronted or because the secret is finally out in the open for others to see?
- What if the abuser abuses me when I confront him—verbally, physically, or even sexually? (This does occasionally happen.)

Such responses by the accused abuser can devastate a woman in recovery.

Then again, when a woman's memories of past abuse are partial or incomplete, she may be tempted to seek additional information or confirmation of the facts, even from her abuser. She may ask herself—

- What really happened?
- Am I remembering the actual facts of what happened, or is my memory faulty?
- Did something else happen that I don't remember?
- Did this happen only once, or did it happen several times over a period of time?

These and other questions may haunt a woman in recovery; answers can be agonizingly slow in coming. Such complicating factors make choosing confrontation difficult. Sometimes confrontation is not even possible if the abuser or abusers are unknown or are no longer living. There are simply no formulas for determining whether to confront.

If a woman *does* decide to confront her abuser, a conservative approach is the best policy. A woman in recovery confronts her abuser in a controlled, supportive environment with the help and participation of a third person, preferably a trained professional counselor or therapist, who acts as moderator and supportive ally. (The woman's husband should definitely *not* be in this role.) The confrontation should be well-rehearsed in advance of the meeting, and the motivation for it should be understood well ahead of time.

A person in recovery should not expect a particular response from the abuser, but should be prepared for any response—including the worst-case scenario. The success or failure of the confrontation rests not with the responses of the person confronted but with the resolve of the confronter.

A woman in recovery places herself at the mercy of her abuser (again) by requiring a certain response from him. To avoid this, the woman's focus should be not the abuser's response, but her own words and feelings during the confrontation. If after the confrontation she can say, "I've said what I needed to say, in the way I needed to say it, and I've placed the appropriate blame for the abuse squarely on the shoulders of the abuser—where it belongs," then she has accomplished a successful confrontation.

But if she needs her abuser to acknowledge what happened, to accept the responsibility for it, and to beg her forgiveness, then she is only setting herself up for tremendous disappointment. A penitent abuser, of course, can work wonders in a woman's healing; but she cannot hope for this.

What this means to a husband is this: *don't pressure your wife either to confront her abuser or to avoid a confrontation*. As difficult as it is to decide what to do, she must decide for herself. The best thing for you to do is wait for her to decide—and then support her decision.

Your wife's forgiveness may not result in the restoration of the original relationship with the abuser. Understand, too, that if your wife's abuser was a family member, she may not want to be around that person—especially if the abuser has not asked her forgiveness. For example, don't think that just because your wife has forgiven him, she feels okay about attending the family reunions and other get-togethers.

Relationships require energy and commitment on the part of both parties. Abusers seldom acknowledge their past sin and persist in denying their actions. In such cases their relationship with the woman they once abused cannot be restored, though she may forgive him. Be sensitive to your wife's needs regarding these issues.

One woman we know who was abused as a child by a neighbor and family friend is now constantly thrust into situations where her parents and siblings invite the abuser to family outings and holiday get-togethers. In spite of the family's full knowledge of the past abuse (though not by the abuser's confession), the family expects this young woman to pretend as if nothing ever happened. To her credit, she refuses to play along with the family charade, choosing instead to spend her holidays elsewhere with friends rather than subject herself to such cruelty.

Husbands of women recovering from past abuse should avoid forcing an unwanted relationship on their wives simply because they have some preconceived notion of what her forgiveness should look like. Don't confuse forgiveness with the restoration of a relationship.

Rebuild

Once your wife has released the anger, bitterness, and resentment of the past, she can rebuild her sense of who she is. After dismantling a false identity and sense of self based on lies, she can begin rebuilding a new and positive self-image based on truth. John was surprised to learn from Jeanne that this was one of the scariest times of her recovery process. "I was terrified," she once told him. "I didn't know who I would turn out to be, and I didn't know if I would like myself—or if you would like me."

Don't confuse an appropriate, positive sense of self based on knowledge and truth (also called self-love) with cheap notions of self-esteem. In *Further Along the Road Less Traveled*, psychiatrist M. Scott Peck distinguishes self-love from self-esteem.

> It's critical for us to be realistic, to have a true knowledge of ourselves as we are, and to be able to recognize both the good parts and the bad parts of ourselves. Further, there is a distinction between self-love and self-esteem, in my opinion. And the difference between self-love (which I propose is a good thing) and self-esteem (which I propose can be a questionable thing) is often confused. . . . Self-love implies the care, respect, and responsibility for and the knowledge of the self. Without loving one's self one cannot love others. But do not confuse self-love with self-centeredness. . . . There is a difference between insisting that we regard ourselves as important (which is self-love) and insisting that we always feel good about ourselves (which is synonymous with constantly preserving our self-esteem). Understanding and making this distinction is crucial to our self-knowledge.[6]

Ever wonder why your wife doesn't believe the truth that she is talented, though you've told her hundreds of times? Chances are, she simply doesn't believe she is talented, or pretty, or a good mother. Abused women seldom accept or internalize compliments or positive messages about them until well into their recovery process. Because of negative internal messages due to the abuse, a woman continues to believe that she is no good. Once your wife begins to rebuild on a good foundation—a new sense of self—tremendous personal growth toward wholeness results.

Growth

Growing up is both exciting and painful at the same time. John remembers that his eyesight gradually deteriorated during his eighth-grade year. He could focus only on things close to him. When he finally mentioned to his parents that much of what he was seeing was blurry, they took him to the doctor to get his vision checked. They learned that he was simply growing rapidly—growth spurts commonly affect a person's eyesight.

In much the same way, as your wife experiences tremendous personal growth within the context of her recovery, she may become so focused on the process that she doesn't seem to notice what's going on around her. It may seem to you like she can see only what's going on in *her* life, and that you and your children are gradually going out of focus. This is especially true if you are used to being taken care of by your wife. Doing things for yourself that she always did for you is uncomfortable and you may feel she is being selfish.

Your wife's inner preoccupation, however, is an important part of her growth toward wholeness. As she grows in her recovery, your own life will become less comfortable and convenient. Your wife may establish healthy boundaries for herself for the first time in her life—a big adjustment for any husband.

Some men don't adjust, however, but continue to view their wives in ways that are detrimental to both of them. If your wife has experienced serious depression, for example, or chronic exhaustion or long periods of withdrawal during her recovery, such circumstances mold your feelings about your wife—and the mold is seldom flattering. Husbands in this situation gradually acquire a negative mental image of their wives as victims. Rather than acknowledge that the abuse happened and that their wives are, with great effort, dealing with it and becoming better people—instead these husbands get the idea that their wives have somehow become less than they were, and that they—the husbands—are the strong ones, more capable than their weak wives who need special care and attention.

In psychological terms, such husbands view their wives as "designated patients"—in other words, people who are *supposed to need* special care, whether or not they actually do.

Such subtle impressions of your wife may be difficult to resist, especially since they are usually formed when you were thrust into the role of care-giver during her recovery. But resist them anyway, for they are *seldom accurate* and *always dangerous* to the long-term health of your marriage relationship.

Confronting the harsh reality of past sexual abuse is a terrifying thing for any person to do. If your wife has the courage to face this challenge, then *weak* is a thoroughly inaccurate word to describe her. To the contrary, it is common for women, when confronted by their past sexual abuse, to rush headlong into the process at a death-defying pace. As one woman said, "I am going to work through this, even if it kills me."

Your wife's recovery process irrevocably changes her in many ways, though not in the ways you anticipate. During this stage don't confuse her temporary *symptoms* with *permanent changes*, which are largely internal and are not readily discernible to you. Only after these long-term changes have aged—changes that affect self-image, confidence, and sense of worth—will you notice anything substantially, positively different about her. The changes are subtle at first, but as she starts to experience the growth and freedom discussed here, you will likely observe an exciting transformation.

With a clearer sense of who she is and a newfound self-confidence, your wife begins to change more rapidly and in more fundamental ways. She exhibits more independence and firmer boundaries in her relationships with you and other people. She is more self-assured and decisive about what she does and doesn't like. She cultivates a hobby or other interests outside the home. She may look for new friendships.

All these changes are healthy and ample evidence of significant growth—though they may not fit your mental image of her.

So reexamine how you view her. Make sure you aren't presuming—falsely and inappropriately—that your wife still needs special care, long after she actually does. An accurate view of who your wife really is, based on present realities instead of past falsehoods, is critical to fostering long-term growth and health in your marriage relationship.

Wholeness

Even with distinct stages, recovery is an ongoing process. In fact, individuals usually go around the recovery circle many times as they heal. Although we have discussed the recovery process only in relation to women who have been sexually abused, the recovery process applies to anyone with emotional wounds or losses.

With each new memory that comes to mind during her recovery, your wife may need to work through each of the stages—again—from reliving the memory to releasing it. Some memories and events may seem to take longer to process than others, but she will always progress from one stage to the next.

When you understand the recovery process, then you can assist your wife as she walks through it—instead of unintentionally throwing up barriers to her healing.

But to become a full-fledged ally, you also need to understand how you may look like an abuser to your wife.

Questions for Thought and Discussion

1. Give examples from your own life of the two kinds of wounds.

2. Think of a difficult loss in your life, and apply these stages of recovery.

3. How have you seen your wife pass through the different stages of the recovery process?

4. How many times have you seen your wife pass through the various stages?

5. Has your wife ever gotten stuck in a stage?

6. What difference does knowing the recovery process make in the relationship between you and your wife?

Chapter Nine
"You Are the Man"

I can't believe the way she treats me." The veins in Larry's neck bulged as he spoke. "You would think *I* was the one who had abused her!"

In his heart if not from his lips, every man I know whose wife is going through the process of recovery from past abuse has spoken these words. It seems unfair for a wife to target her husband with anger that is more appropriately directed toward the man who abused her. Why should a woman's husband pay the price for a past abuser's actions?

Yet the lines between past abuse and a husband's present actions are not that distinct. We know this isn't easy for a husband to hear. For this chapter to make sense, we recommend that you read it from beginning to end in a single sitting.

"How Dare You Blame Me!"

Ancient Israel's King David, enthralled by the beauty of Bathsheba, committed adultery with her. Upon discovering she was pregnant as a result of their tryst, David tried to cover his tracks by calling her husband back from the battle in hopes he would sleep with his wife. But Uriah—a man of integrity, faithfulness, duty—refused to sleep with Bathsheba as long as his fellow soldiers remained on the front lines. David saw no way to save his own reputation except to order Uriah murdered on the battlefront so that the king was free to marry Uriah's widow.

About a year later the prophet Nathan made his way to the king's throne room. Under the guise of seeking the king's wisdom regarding a point of law, he narrated what David took to be recent news in Israel.

A poor man in the kingdom had but one ewe lamb, and he loved it like a daughter. Recently this poor man's neighbor came pounding on his door. He was entertaining guests, and though he had many sheep and goats himself with which to prepare a meal, he took this poor man's one ewe and slaughtered it for his feast.

Nathan was interrupted by David's angry outburst: "As the Lord lives, surely the man who has done this deserves to die. And he must make restitution for the lamb fourfold, because he did this thing and had no compassion."

Nathan looked the king straight in the eye. "You are the man!" he declared.

Like David, husbands of wives who have been abused may righteously denounce abuse—despite the fact that they talk to and behave in much the same way as their wives' abusers. It is ironic that such husbands ask angrily, "How can my wife treat me like I was her abuser?" But these men need a Nathan to point his finger at them, look them in the eye, and say, "You are the man!" Although this statement may feel like a slap in the face, prompting you to close the book on this chapter, a significant act of preserving your marriage may be your honest acknowledgment that some of your actions resemble those of your wife's abuser in ways we will suggest. Ultimately, recognizing this may be the key to crafting a more satisfying relationship with your wife.

A man's sexual abuse of a little girl consists of forcing his will upon her—against her will and without her approval—for his own gratification. He demands from her what will give him pleasure.

During her recovery from past abuse, your wife relives awful memories as part of her healing. She remembers how much she hated that man for how he used her. She remembers wishing she were big enough to make him stop. She remembers feeling cheap and painfully helpless.

It only makes sense, then, that when her husband says or does anything that even loosely resembles abusive behavior, a wife instantly responds with rage and indignation. Many men whose wives have been abused report that they feel like their wife is taking out on them all of her rage and hostility from her past.

One reason husbands are often targeted is that they are the ones present when the emotions and events of a woman's past come to life. Another reason is that *without knowing it, husbands say and do things that make their wife feel abused all over again*. If she feels like you are forcing your will on her for your pleasure and at her expense, she will thoroughly and fiercely resist you. She will fire on you with all her emotional energy.

One man remembers an incident when his wife was in the early stages of her recovery. As soon as he arrived home, he told her he had to leave again in an hour to attend an evening meeting he had forgotten to mention to her that morning. He asked when dinner would be ready.

He might as well have told her he was leaving town with another woman. She abruptly began slamming her way through the house, verbally assaulting him until his blood boiled.

Why the instant, violent reaction? It so happened that she was at the stage in her recovery process of reliving the most vivid, anxiety-producing memories of what it felt like to be used for someone else's selfish pleasures. She was remembering how horrible it felt to have someone force his will on her without regard for her feelings. To her, her husband's spur-of-the-moment request for an early supper felt exactly the same as her past abuse. She heard in his request, "What you're doing is unimportant compared to my desires—so get my dinner ready."

Was he forcing his will upon her? No. Was he using her selfishly? Not intentionally. But that's how she felt. Unfortunately, sometimes her perception is accurate—he *is* using her selfishly. Her reaction, related as it was to her past abuse, exacted a price from her husband for what someone else had done to her long ago. No, it's not fair—but it's reality.

To be fair, women in recovery from past abuse know intellectually that since their husbands are not their abusers of the past, they are not the ones who should pay the price for what those abusers did to them. But in the midst of recovery, it's difficult to separate the feelings of the past from the events of the present. Deep emotional wounds surface that, when touched by some word or action by their husband, cause an explosion.

Sometimes you may end up the target of your wife's rage simply because you are the most significant male in her life. If her abuser was a father, brother, uncle, or close family friend (male), she may be sensitive to anything that you do or say that feels abusive to her. But even if she didn't perceive as significant the man who violated her, your gender alone may qualify you as representative of all men who use women for their gratification.

Behaving as an Abuser

It may puzzle you that, after five or ten or twenty years of doing and saying the same sorts of things in the same way—with nary a raised eyebrow from your wife—today you get blasted for it. This occurs because a woman who has been sexually abused often doesn't even recognize, much less defend herself against, inappropriate words and actions of others—including her husband. So without a reaction from his wife, a husband's words and behavior may over time erect destructive patterns of interaction with his wife.

But sooner or later it breaks. As a woman begins working through her recovery process, she learns to interact honestly

with her husband and others. She no longer tolerates unde-
served criticism or the selfish, hurtful acts of others. In your
defense, you may not even realize you're acting selfishly or offering inappropriate criticism—until she confronts you with it. Her
touchiness may cause you to feel you can't get away with *anything* anymore. In the ensuing barrage of hostility, you get the
sense that all the rules of the game have been suddenly
changed—but no one told you about it.

Husbands commonly act in four ways that make their
wives feel as if their men are forcing their will upon her—like
she's being abused all over again. Especially when a woman recovering from her past abuse is in the stage of reliving her memories,
these situations can quickly escalate into open warfare.

Forcing Your Will Sexually.

While you might wish it to be otherwise, if your wife is at
the stage in recovering from past sexual abuse where she is
remembering the sexual advances of a past abuser, any sexual
advance you make may feel like abuse to her. She couldn't repel
her abuser's advance back then, but she's now capable of
repelling your advance—and she'll probably do just that.

Even approaching her for simply a hug or a kiss may feel
to your wife like you are forcing your will upon her for your own
benefit. Of course you feel completely rejected by her. But pushing for a hug she doesn't feel comfortable responding to isn't
worth it for you. Your insistence, instead of being interpreted as
loving desire for her, will be perceived as abuse. You risk further,
possibly violent rejection and damage to your marriage that is
not easily repaired.

Some husbands confronted with this dilemma make a
choice to win, so they force their will upon their wife in spite of
her protests. This is inexcusable, manifest abuse. The typical
woman in recovery won't stay indefinitely in a situation where
her husband has chosen to win at the expense of her feelings. It
simply feels like more abuse.

As unfair as it seems, we must adapt to our wife's changes from stage to stage along her road to recovery. Though the end result is worth it, the process is tortuous for her and for you. The Bible puts it well when it tells husbands to "be considerate as you live with your wives" (1 Peter 3:7). We are considerate when we honor and respect them by not pushing to get what we want sexually.

We are not, however, advocating choosing to lose. Giving up and denying your own sexual needs without your saying anything is not helpful. But understand that your sexual advances may feel abusive to her. Serious and straightforward communication about your sexual relationship, and each other's sexual needs, is critical for the marriage to survive.

Applying Conditional Love.

Another way that we may resemble our wife's abuser is by placing conditions on our love. Twisted and unhealthy dynamics allow prolonged abuse to continue. Case in point: an abuser tells a little girl that as long as she lets him do what he wants to do to her, he will love her. But if she resists him or ever tells anyone, then he will no longer love her. A young girl who experiences such evil manipulation learns at an early age that love is conditional. During her recovery, therefore, that woman is irritable about *anything* her husband does that appears to her to be conditional love. If your wife feels that your love is in any way conditional, she may react forcefully.

Discouraging Her Counseling.

Husbands appear like abusers when they discourage their wives' counseling. Say you observe that matters get worse the more she goes to therapy; so you suggest, "Honey, it seems like you are having such a hard time with your counseling—why not give it a rest for a while?"

To her ears, this says, "I don't like the way things have been changing around here since you started counseling, and I would prefer things to go back to the way they were." His motivation seems to her pure selfishness, not compassion. She perceives his comments as an attempt to force his will upon her for his benefit.

Again, that perception by a wife may be unfortunately accurate. Her husband may indeed be tired of the struggle and want it to end. Ending counseling seems like the quick way to make their own lives easier. But if your wife is truly misreading your behavior and words, then learn new ways to communicate with her without stepping on these land mines.

Covering Up "The Secret."

We behave like an abuser when we keep our wife's abuse a secret from those who can be of help to her. In an effort to guard a wife's privacy about her past, a well-meaning husband may say something like this: "You know, honey, it might be best if we didn't tell anyone about your past abuse." He congratulates himself for being sensitive—but to his wife, it's the same old message she heard during her past abuse: "We won't tell anyone about our little secret, will we?"

If secrecy surrounded her past abuse, she can't help but believe that the reason you don't want anyone to know about it is your own selfish concern—embarrassment over marrying a victim of childhood sexual abuse, a hypocritical desire to hide marital struggles, guilt about some of the ways you *do* force your will upon your wife for your benefit. Whatever the reason, suggesting that the abuse shouldn't be discussed outside of the home usually receives a negative reaction. Realize that she interprets your behavior and communication through the grid of her painfully present past. If you push the button that reverberates with the feelings and events of her past sexual abuse, you will get the full force of the emotions that are associated with that long-gone but not-forgotten event.

Behaving as an Accomplice

If you think, however, that your best defense against unexpected rage is silence, think again. There are other players in your wife's past: accomplices, those who knew about your wife's abuse—or should have known about it—and yet did nothing to prevent or stop it. One or both of your wife's parents may have been an accomplice.

Imagine this common scenario: a little girl tells her mother about the things that Daddy does to her in the dark when Mommy isn't home. Mommy tells the child that such imaginations are bad and that Daddy would never do anything like that to his little girl. She reprimands her daughter for telling vicious lies. Mommy doesn't believe her daughter, never checks it out—and the abuse continues. The little girl quickly learns that you can't trust *anyone* to help you, not even when you confide in a parent.

The mothers of children being abused have often themselves been abused in the past. If they have not dealt with their own abuse, they may be unable to help their daughter deal with hers. They either don't know how to respond or respond passively, casting themselves in the role of accomplice. Some mothers so deny or repress the memory of their own abuse that the abuse of their daughter seems as unreal to them as their own abuse. They are blind to the abuse that is taking place and thus unwittingly become accomplices.

Other possible accomplices: school counselors, youth pastors, coaches—*if* they take no action on a young girl's report of abuse, or if they disbelieve her. The youth pastor who glibly advises a teenage girl, "You are supposed to honor your parents, so do what they tell you to do"—this youth pastor is an accomplice in the girl's mind. This youth pastor effectively told the young girl that God wants her to submit to abuse at the hands of her parents.

Formerly aborted cries for help are today much more

likely to be assured a hearing and investigation. Counselors, teachers, and clergy *must* report potential abuse, according to the law. Yet most recovering women we know were abused before such requirements were in place, and many of them can recite the name of a counselor, teacher, or a pastor who was told about the abuse, but who did nothing about it. Those authority figures are accomplices to the abuse because their inaction allowed the abuse to continue unabated.

Other accomplices to the abuse are those people whom the young girl feared to approach because of the expected negative reaction she would receive. She should have been able to go to these people for help, but instead she felt paralyzed with fear. Maybe the accomplice was an angry and critical mother who had a way of making things the fault of her daughter—your wife. Your wife may have thought that if she went to her mother with this secret, she would be made to feel even more guilty than she already did. Maybe another accomplice was a too-busy father, who had such a distant relationship with his little girl that she couldn't possibly bring up such a frightening subject. In this case, she didn't know him well enough to know how he would react, so she didn't tell him.

Finally, *you* may play the part of an accomplice in your wife's perception, because of what you say (or don't say) or do (or don't do). Remembering those people who knew about her abuse but did nothing to stop it or to help her, she may believe you are saying and doing the same things.

You can appear like an accomplice to your wife in at least four ways.

Denying Her Abuse.

More than one husband has secretly (or even openly) wondered whether the abuse ever actually occurred; maybe his wife just made it all up. If you doubt the reality of your wife's abuse, she will associate you with that other person she confided in a long time ago who didn't believe her. The anger that your wife reserves for the person who knew about the abuse and did nothing about it is unleashed on you when you say the same things or act the same way as that person.

Since you can't personally verify the facts of your wife's abuse, the only reasonable alternative is to believe them to be true. Whatever doubts you have about details, keep them to yourself—for to deny her abuse is to play the part of an accomplice.

Minimizing Her Pain.

"It's not that bad, sweetheart," she heard from a trusted adult when she was a child. "Everything will be all right." Like any of us, a woman who has been abused seeks to be taken seriously and to have her feelings validated. She knows how horrifying her experience felt to her. She knows how frightened and angry she was. She knows how violated and disgusted she felt. For a husband to minimize her pain just to calm her down benefits neither of them. She needs to feel the full force of her feelings in order to work through them.

If you come riding in on your white horse and try to save this damsel in distress by minimizing her pain, she will likely rise up and rip you out of your saddle with her bare hands. During your wife's recovery she needs you to validate her emotions, to agree with her that her feelings are appropriate. (We discuss in chapter 11 how you can do this.)

Implying Her Guilt.

Husbands sometimes play the role of an accomplice by implying their wife's guilt in her past abuse. Some husbands can't believe childhood sexual abuse could ever happen. They can't picture themselves ever engaging in something so hideous, and they can't imagine anyone else doing anything like that, either—unless the victim did something to ask for it.

If in your heart you think this, you will inevitably communicate it by insinuation. "Did your dad see you running around the house naked, or flirting with him—is that why he

did this to you?" you may ask your wife. The obvious implica-
tion is that your wife did something to cause the abuser to
behave as he did.

A variation on implied guilt is a husband who, probing
for details about his wife's abuse, asks, "Didn't you do anything
to make him stop? Why didn't you lock the door or tell someone?" The husband questions his wife's judgment when he asks
questions that all start with "Why didn't you. . . ." The implica-
tion is that if your wife didn't do something to make her abuser
stop, then she handled the situation wrongly.

Such detailed questioning implies guilt on her part. If you
are busy implying guilt while she is fighting to find freedom
from false guilt by reinterpreting what happened, she won't tol-
erate your curiosity for long.

Even if a young girl *did* do something that her abuser perceived as seductive, he must accept the full responsibility for
choosing to act on his perceptions and take advantage of the situation. Everyone is responsible for how he or she behaves.
Outside forces may press in on a man right up to the point of
decision, but he alone decides how he will act. Someone may
enrage you, but it is you alone who decides to punch him in the
nose.

We need to wholeheartedly be on our wife's side, affirm-
ing that she was not to blame and that her abuser was the only
guilty party. In reality, girls at the age when typically abused, are
seldom sophisticated enough to understand how to seduce, even
if they wanted to.

Playing a Passive Role in Her Recovery.

The defining characteristic of accomplices is passivity—
when they should have done something, they didn't. When they
should have believed her, they didn't. When they should have
validated her emotions and helped her, they didn't. When they
should have confronted the offender, they instead made her feel
guilty.

Sid remembers when Nancy brought home a video tape about recovering from past sexual abuse. He was exceptionally busy, so it wasn't until a week later that they got around to watching it. The pace of the material was a little slow, and before he knew it, he fell asleep.

To Nancy his behavior had only one meaning: "I'm not all that interested in your healing." To her Sid looked like an accomplice from her past—and she proceeded to let him know about it, in no uncertain terms. And rightfully so! Sid admits that the moment he began to get sleepy, he should have stopped the tape and communicated his sincere interest in viewing it with her, restating his commitment to her recovery process. Then he should have admitted he was starting to get sleepy and suggested that they finish it at another time when he could give the tape his full attention—which he really wanted to do.

Here's the rub. If you take the bull by the horns and try to assist your wife, you run the danger of looking like an abuser who wants to force your will upon her for your benefit. She may perceive your efforts as an attempt to push her toward healing so that *your* life can get back to normal.

On the other hand, if you back off and play a more passive role, she may see you as an accomplice and accuse you of not caring enough for her to travel the painful road of recovery with her. Can you ever win?

You may already know how it feels to look like an abuser one day and an accomplice the next. How you can walk this fine line—trying to help, but not forcing your way—we address in the next chapter.

Questions for Thought and Discussion

1. In which of the ways listed (forcing your will sexually, applying conditional love, discouraging her counseling, covering up the secret) can you see that you have said or done things that may have reminded your wife of her abuse or abuser?

2. Are there other ways you have forced your will upon your wife for your own benefit?

3. In which of the ways listed (denying her abuse, minimizing her pain, implying her guilt, playing a passive role in her recovery) have you acted like an accomplice?

4. Are there other ways you have acted like an accomplice?

5. Is it hard to admit that you have behaved like an abuser or an accomplice?

Chapter Ten
Playing Your Position

The man whose wife is recovering from past sexual abuse must understand his role in his wife's recovery process. Playing an inappropriate role or responding in a way that used to be but is no longer appropriate can subvert a woman's healing process.

You see the importance of appropriate roles in football games all the time. A talented quarterback drops back into the pocket, throws a beautiful thirty-five-yard spiral with pinpoint accuracy—to empty turf. Not a receiver within ten yards. Or a running back takes the hand-off and heads for the slot—but the guard pulls to the wrong side, leaving his ball-carrier facing several hungry defensive linemen. For the running back the play holds no gain, but only pain.

So it is with the husband who either plays the wrong role or who does the wrong things during his wife's recovery—no gain, only pain. There is a better way.

In this chapter we lay the foundation for understanding your role in your wife's recovery from past abuse. Then in chapters 11 and 12, we discuss the details of playing your position well.

On Being a Husband

Defining your role demands rethinking what it means to be a husband. When a man asked me how he could survive his wife's recovery from her past sexual abuse, I answered with a question. "Tell me, Dave—what do you think it means to be a husband?"

His grin told me he thought it an easy question. "A husband is the one who provides, protects, and sets the pace for his family."

"As long as you maintain that definition of a husband," I replied, "you'll face nothing but more pain in your marriage."

A husband by Dave's definition is playing his position in a way that sets him up for conflict with a wife in recovery from past abuse.

Being a Provider Can Backfire.

A man generally takes his role of provider seriously. He works hard to make ends meet and thinks he's playing his position well if he can pay the mortgage, buy the kids school clothes, and keep a couple of cars in the driveway.

His wife, however, looks at it a bit differently. Her husband works hard all day, comes home, lands in the recliner, and hides behind the newspaper until he's called for dinner. In short, she sees an accomplice in his passivity toward her recovery. To her, being *taken care of* is not being *cared about*. A man who thinks his position as husband is defined only by providing financially for his family feels hurt and confused when his wife doesn't appear to appreciate him for all he does. His pain places even greater strain on a relationship that's already tense.

Being a Protector Can Backfire.

Today's widely accepted definition of a husband goes far beyond merely providing for the financial needs of his family. Men also view themselves as protectors. Yet a protector may inadvertently look like an abuser to his wife.

Because Greg loved Jill, he constantly tried to protect her from harm. Knowing she had been sexually abused in the past, he wanted to ensure that nothing like that would ever again happen to the love of his life. Assuring himself that he had her best interests in mind, he didn't allow his wife to go shopping by herself for fear that someone would accost her in the parking lot. Afraid that some man might cast a lustful glance in her direction, Greg limited her wardrobe to only those items that met his approval. When he infrequently did allow her to go out alone, she had to let him know exactly when she would be back.

In short, she became a virtual prisoner in her own home, waiting for her husband to accompany her on short excursions of freedom.

When Jill began actively dealing with her past abuse, she began perceiving her protective husband as an abuser because he forced his will upon her. Greg thought he was only playing his position of protector well; to Jill, protector was the wrong position for him to play—and they experienced intense seasons of conflict and pain.

Being a Pace Setter Can Backfire.

A man who thinks setting the pace is key to his husbanding can also end up looking like an abuser to his wife. She may interpret his leadership only as an attempt to force his will on her. Instead of peace, there's only more pain—and everyone loses.

The longer you hold to providing, protecting, and setting the pace as the definition of your role as a husband, the more likely you are to run headlong into serious conflict with a wife who is recovering from past sexual abuse.

Yet changing your understanding of the position you play is very difficult. Our culture largely defines a modern husband's role. To personally redefine your husbanding, then, can feel like stripping yourself of manhood. Can we even picture what it means to be a husband without invoking provision, protection, and leadership?

Our belief system also lies behind our understanding of the roles and responsibilities of a husband. To some Christian men, altering the traditional definition of a husband feels unbiblical. They're quick to quote Scripture to prove their stance: "If anyone does not provide for his relatives, and especially for his immediate family, he has denied the faith and is worse than an unbeliever" (1 Tim. 5:8). Such men remind us that our wives are the "weaker partner" according to the apostle Peter (1 Peter 3:7), and thus must be protected. They quote the apostle Paul to affirm their role as leader: "Wives, submit to your husbands as to the Lord. For the husband is the head of the wife as Christ is the head of the church" (Eph. 5:22–23).

It is undeniable that among a husband's marital responsibilities are those of providing, protecting, and leading. But limiting yourself to these roles is overly simplistic. Following traditionally defined roles of a husband as one would a formula can be especially counterproductive in this context. Ultimately, God himself is the provider, protector, and leader of his people—including wives. Interjecting yourself between your wife and God as the *sole* provider-protector-leader in your family is essentially elevating yourself, godlike, over your wife.

Men who elevate themselves to such a position believe that only they can provide what their wives need. Their suspicion can prevent counselors and close friends from playing important roles in their wives' recovery. They believe that only they know what their wives need protection from. They demand that their wives stop seeing a counselor who, in a husband's short-sightedness, seems to be making things worse rather than better. Or they may superintend their wives to such a suffocating degree that she feels abused all over again. They assume the role of counselor, advising their wives throughout the recovery process. Granted, many of these men provide, protect, and lead their wives in a sincere desire to help them; but they are blind to the harm they actually cause when they don't clearly distinguish their roles from God's roles.

Any time we place ourselves in a position over our wives that is reserved for God, we bargain for greater pain for everyone. The process of recovery is best facilitated when you let God be God to your wife—and when you stick to your own position.

Instead of interjecting yourself between your wife and God, recognize that she has a direct relationship with God. That means encouraging her to seek God for *his* provision for her needs, *his* protection of her well-being, *his* leadership in the affairs of her life. The last thing you need is to be your wife's god.

Since most views of what it means to be a husband are deeply entrenched in our culture and our belief system, any attempt to redefine the role of a husband is like running into the wind. We can't transform single-handedly an entire culture's definition of *man* and *husband*. Neither do we wish to undermine a person's beliefs about providing, protecting, and setting the pace in the family. Such duties are, after all, legitimate aspects of biblical husbanding.

All we want is to demonstrate that adapting to a wife who is recovering from past sexual abuse demands that we focus on one of the most commonly overlooked aspects of what it means to be a husband—being your wife's friend.

On Being a Friend

A friend travels the road of life with you. A friend is a companion who comes alongside of you to walk with you. Friends don't push you to go in a certain direction against your will, nor do they hold you back from going where you want or need to go. Friends keep pace with you step for step; they don't try to play God in your life; they simply commit themselves to traveling with you wherever God leads you.

God demonstrated that friendship is an ingredient in his definition of a husband when he observed that "it is not good for the man to be alone," determining to make a helper suitable for him (Gen. 2:18). Notice that leadership, provision, and protection didn't show up in God's original blueprint for marriage; he rather made someone who would end man's loneliness and be a suitable helper for him. The accomplishing of man's divinely ordained purpose in this world was meant to be conducted in a partnership. No sense of hierarchy here. Just companionship.

This biblical understanding of marriage is reiterated in the Song of Solomon, which celebrates God's ideal in marital love. The bride says about her husband, "This is my lover, this is my friend" (Song 5:16). From God's vantage, marriage is the ultimate expression of friendship.

So precious is this companionship in marriage, and so much a part of God's design for marriage, that in the Old Testament book of Malachi he condemned his people for violating their companionship with each other. In a scathing rebuke the prophet chastised God's people: "The LORD is acting as the witness between you and the wife of your youth, because you have broken faith with her, though she is your partner, the wife of your marriage covenant" (Mal. 2:14). Clearly, God intends husbands to be companions and friends to their wives.

Friends Understand and Care.

Being your wife's friend has implications for how you interact with her during her recovery. Friends understand each other. Being a friend to your wife means you follow the biblical injunction to "be considerate as you live with your wives" (1 Peter 3:7). You do your best to understand the influences of her past on her—which incidentally protects you from falling into the role of accomplice, that uninterested, uncaring person in your wife's past. If you demonstrate interest in who she is, what she's gone through, and what she's going through now, your relationship with her will be active but not pushy.

Showing interest *doesn't* mean sitting her down after her counseling session and demanding that she tell you everything. Friends don't force each other to divulge personal and painful information; they wait to be told. You communicate your desire to walk with your wife through her highs and lows. You let her know you'll be there for her when she needs you. You create a safe climate within which she can reveal more of herself to you, thereby opening additional opportunities for you to be supportive.

You honor your wife by shaping your behavior in ways that say, "I care about you. I want to understand and be supportive of you." You admire her for the precious treasure she is. A woman who years ago was used by a man to gratify his own selfish desires—this adult woman now thrives in her recovery when she finds herself in the arms of her husband who is considerate of her by living with her as an understanding friend.

She's not the only one who directly benefits from this approach. The apostle Peter mentions a reward for those husbands who live with their wives in such a fashion: an unhindered prayer life (1 Peter 3:7).

Friends Make Personal Sacrifices.

Friends respect each other. Friends don't run roughshod over each other by forcing their will on each other. Again the Bible clearly instructs a husband how to be his wife's friend: "Husbands, love your wives, just as Christ loved the church and gave himself up for her. . . . In this same way, husbands ought to love their wives as their own bodies" (Eph. 5:25, 28). Rather than demanding that your wife fall in line behind you, love your wife to the point of personal sacrifice.

Sid reached a point during his wife's recovery where he had to make a decision. Would he make some additional sacrifices on her behalf or not? As it was, he had already made considerable sacrifices: He committed finacially to her counseling, tried to be supportive, came home early to care for their boys whenever she went to counseling (though it meant making up lost time later). Yet instead of appreciating his sacrifices, she vented on him all her pent-up emotions from her past abuse.

To make matters worse, she began demanding even *more* from him—help with housecleaning, assistance in dinner preparations, scheduling with her well in advance any plans he wanted to make. He didn't know if he could give any more—or even if he wanted to.

He was away at a planning retreat when he felt strongly that he had to choose between requiring Nancy to submit to him as her husband and do things his way, or make further sacrifices to help a hurting friend—who happened to be his wife.

Sid chose the latter, and he's glad he did. It was a turning point in their relationship and in her recovery. She began to see the difference between a man who used her and one who loved her. It wasn't magic, but rather Sid's *conscious choice to be her friend,* which entailed making some personal sacrifices for her.

Providing support and assistance even at the cost of personal sacrifice is an important element in any healthy marriage or friendship. Sid's wife had provided this for him at other times during their life together, and he realized that she needed this from him now. Understanding and sacrifice create the climate in which real healing can occur.

A husband creates a climate in which his wife can find healing—like a sign at a medical office reminded me. Outside, near the door to the waiting room, was a large sign that instructed patients with fever and rash to go to a different room to check in. The clinic administrators knew they had to maintain a climate in which healing could take place—and that highly contagious people sitting in an enclosed waiting room only compounded existing health problems.

The husband who creates a climate in which his wife can find healing concentrates on his role as his wife's friend and downplays his more traditional roles. He puts more energy into understanding what she's going through and making appropriate sacrifices than into protecting, providing, and setting the pace. He never wholly abandons these other roles, of course, but when it comes to relating to his wife, his primary role is that of her closest friend.

As we say in our seminar, "Be your wife's friend, not her

husband." In other words, stop being all of those things that husbands are commonly thought to be. Be her friend instead. Then you both win.

Now let's think about how to effectively play the role of friend.

Questions for Thought and Discussion

1. What does it mean to you to be a husband?

2. In what ways have providing, protecting, and leading caused problems in your marriage?

3. How does the idea of being your wife's friend differ from your idea of being her husband?

4. If you were to be your wife's friend, what changes would you have to make in your present lifestyle?

5. Explain how being your wife's friend and not her husband will help her in her recovery from past abuse.

Chapter Eleven
Communicating Terms of Peace

One of the most powerful things you can do in your wife's recovery process is to communicate that you want to be your wife's ally. Her acceptance of that well-communicated desire establishes the climate for significant healing. But communicating such a message can be one of the most difficult things a man may ever have to do.

Men can be notoriously poor communicators. Cartoonist Gary Larson portrays Tarzan rehearsing his first words to Jane. He tries "How do you do? My name is Tarzan, and I believe you are known as Jane." Then a more formal approach: "Allow me to introduce myself. I am Tarzan, Lord of the Jungle. And you?" He tries the casual approach: "You must be Jane. I am Tarzan. It's a pleasure to meet you." When the moment of truth arrives and Jane is standing before him, in spite of all his rehearsals of impressive introductions, what comes out is "Me Tarzan. You Jane." He covers his face in embarrassment, muttering under his breath, "Damn!"

It isn't that men have nothing to say or that they intend to be insensitive in what they say. It's just that for some reason the words don't come out quite right. This is especially true when it comes to expressing our feelings.

Our inability to communicate well can hinder us from being a true friend to our hurting wife, but it doesn't have to be an insurmountable obstacle. We can learn to communicate effectively with our wives. As a skilled counselor and friend of mine says, "Good communication involves two things—knowing what to say, and having the right motive when you say it."

I agree. So let's consider both of these aspects of good communication—*what* to say and *why* we should say it.

What to Say

To create the climate of healing in your marriage, you must communicate three important messages. Properly communicated, these messages can help lay the foundation for a whole new relationship based upon trust.

Make a Confession.

This is simply acknowledging that you have done something that has caused your wife pain. In this context it means confessing to your wife that you have acted like her abuser or like an accomplice, and that your actions resulted in her being hurt.

"Wait a minute," you say. "You have it backwards. *She's* the one who's been hurting *me*. She's the one who's been treating me like dirt, slicing me up with her tongue, and rejecting me with a cold shoulder. When she apologizes, *then* I'll think about doing the same."

Your wife may indeed be guilty of all your charges. But suspend your indignation long enough to acknowledge that you may also be guilty of her charges. Keep in mind that if your wife's explosive negative reactions have been precipitated by her perception that you resemble an abuser or accomplice, then as painful as it may be for you now, *her accusations are positive signs of your wife's growth toward wholeness*.

Think about it. She has resisted you because you have been acting in ways that feel abusive to her or in ways that make you look like an accomplice. Isn't an explosive negative reaction exactly the kind of response we would expect of someone who has a firm sense of identity and appropriate boundaries when she is confronted with a would-be abuser? To go a step further, isn't this the kind of response you *want* her to have?

Imagine this. Your wife is home by herself. Her past abuser rings the doorbell and waits. Your wife opens the door as far as the chain lock will allow. She instantly recognizes him. "I'm back," he says with a smile.

What should your wife do?

A. Scream as loud as she can, slam and dead-bolt the door, and call the police.
B. Stand there in the doorway while her eyes glaze over with resignation, and open the door without uttering a word.
C. Point the barrel of a shotgun out the door and blow the creep away.

You probably chose A or C, both of which are explosive, negative reactions to a potentially abusive situation. (The authors strongly dissuade readers from employing option C—though it sure brings our point home.)

Now recall some of the recent incidents in your marriage in which you were on the receiving end of explosive negative responses from your wife. You need to realize that to her it may have seemed as if her abuser had dropped in for a visit—but in *your* body. With that in mind, maybe you can begin to understand some of her negative responses toward you. It would certainly be ideal if she realized you were not her abuser and handled her anger differently, but maybe her explosions in your direction are less a response to you than an expression of her own inner pain. In any case, she can hardly figure it all out. In reality she may be unable to pinpoint the cause of her negative reaction, let alone communicate how to defuse the situation.

The point is that one of you needs to establish a climate of healing. Why not exercise true leadership now and get the relationship back on the right track? If both of you are waiting for the other one to initiate confession, your relationship will remain stuck in the present pain.

If you've acted in a self-serving manner, forcing your will upon her for your own benefit, then you need to acknowledge that you've treated her very much as an abuser treated her. If you've stood by like an uninvolved spectator, watching her experience pain without being there for her physically and emotionally when she needed you most, you must acknowledge that you've acted much like an accomplice.

And your confession cannot be feigned. You can't water down the message, even though it's hard to say, "I know that I have done many things that have hurt you." The biggest hindrance to making a confession is probably your pride. We hate to admit we've done something wrong, especially when we didn't mean to cause any pain.

Occasionally one of Sid's children accidentally hurts the other one while playing, or says something in jest that hurts the other's feelings. He and Nancy teach them that even if they didn't mean to hurt their sibling, they still need to apologize. But they chafe at the thought of saying what needs to be said when they didn't hurt the other "on purpose." The rules of mending relationships are no different as adults. Even though you may not intentionally hurt your wife, if you want to restore your relationship with her, a confession is in order.

Even when we know it's the right and necessary thing to do, we hate to do it. Perhaps we're afraid to give our wives something to hold over us when it seems they're already beating us over the head with our personal weaknesses or mistakes. Who in his right mind would give the enemy more ammunition? Confessing their hurtful behavior to their wives makes some men feel they're only giving her a whip. Before she could hit them with just her hand, but now she really has something to lash them with.

Granted, confession is risky. If you communicate your message effectively, however (and we will discuss how to do this), your wife may see your sincerity and begin to lower the drawbridge for you to cross the moat she has built to protect herself from further pain. No woman recovering from past abuse drops her guard until she is convinced that she can trust us and that we indeed have her best interest in mind. So the choice is between creating a climate that can bring healing, or living in a stand-off with your wife, waiting for her to make the next move. For some men, unfortunately, the next move their wife makes is to move out.

Express Your Sorrow.

If confessing your wrongdoing was hard, expressing your feelings may be even more difficult.

What feelings do you need to express to her? Perhaps first of all you need to express your genuine sorrow over having caused her pain. It's one thing to acknowledge you have caused her pain; it's another matter to express genuine sorrow for your behavior. To create the climate for healing, you not only need to acknowledge in your mind that you have done many things wrong in dealing with the situation, but you must also communicate—*using your emotions*—the sorrow you feel for the pain you have caused.

This is difficult to do, because you're probably in pain yourself. Most men whose wives are in recovery from past abuse are hurting. Their lives are turned upside down. The women they thought they knew are changing before their eyes. What may have been a satisfying relationship suddenly sours. In the midst of such personal trauma, it's difficult for a man to consider his wife's pain long enough to find much compassion or sympathy for her. But we must do it. For if we try to communicate our confession without compassion, what we say to our wives sounds hollow to them. We may say the right words, but they can tell if our hearts aren't in it. If you want to speak to your wife's heart, then you must speak from your own heart.

To express genuine sorrow, first get in touch with your wife's pain. To do that, get in touch with your *own* emotional pain. When was the last time you cried? Can you even remember it? Can you recall the pain that brought you to tears?

Some men's emotional pain is related to a loss they experienced—a parent's untimely death or the loss of a child, for example. Or maybe it's the pain of wanting a father's love, but never receiving it. Some men remember the pain of rejection they felt in a relationship, or the pain of suffering a failure in life—being driven to bankruptcy or being bypassed for an important promotion. Maybe your pain is exactly the same kind of pain your wife knows, because you were also abused. If a man can recall some of his own emotional wounds and the deep pain associated with them, then he can begin feeling the pain he may have caused his wife—the kind of pain for which he is sorry.

Another way to get in touch with your wife's pain is to imagine the trauma she must have experienced during the period of time she was being abused. Can you picture your wife as a sweet and innocent child, being taken advantage of by an overpowering individual? Can you feel her violation? Her revulsion? Can you hear her crying herself to sleep? Can you sense her confusion? Can you hear her pleading for this to stop? Can you feel her frustration over not being able to make him quit? Can you experience how afraid she is to risk telling someone what's going on? Can you relate to her feelings of guilt or of being dirty or unworthy?

If you can begin to imagine the pain your wife is feeling and then realize that some of the things you have done in your relationship with her feel *just the same* to her, then you are nearing the moment when you can communicate your confession to her from your heart, not just your head. Indeed, when the head and the heart connect, your communication can be profound.

When you communicate from your heart, the difference isn't so much in the words you use as in the way you look at her, the tone of your voice, and the sincerity she hears in your words.

Along with confession and an expression of sorrow, one final ingredient must go into the words you say to your wife—a declaration of your commitment to her.

Declare Your Commitment.

This may be the easiest of the three messages: communicating your commitment to be her ally, not her enemy. It's simply telling her that you want to be on her side, that you don't want to hurt her anymore, and that instead of fighting her, you want to be her friend.

If confession is speaking from your mind, and if expressing your sorrow is speaking from your heart, then declaring your commitment to be her ally is speaking from your will. You communicate not only that you understand what you've done to hurt her and the sorrow you feel because of the hurt you have caused, but also what you've determined to do to be her friend rather than her enemy in the days to come.

Our experience dictates that the most effective way to communicate that commitment is by being as specific as possible. In effect, you are communicating the terms of peace.

When Sid told Nancy he wanted to be her ally, he told her specifically that when he got home from work he would ask her what he could do to help her get dinner prepared (thus avoiding giving her the sense that he was using her for his own benefit by expecting her to have dinner on the table). He told her that he would write all of his meetings and appointments on her calendar as far in advance as possible, so that she wouldn't be unpleasantly surprised at the last minute and feel like he expected her to take care of everything else so that he could do whatever he wanted. Sid also communicated very specifically about how he would change his behavior in their sexual relationship so that she would not feel used. He was specific in communicating to her that he understood what had hurt her, that he was sincerely sorry for the things he had done which caused her pain, and that he was going to do his best to change those things and be her friend, not her enemy.

Any man who wants to get serious about becoming his wife's friend during her recovery from past abuse communicates these three messages to his wife: your confession, your expression of sorrow over having caused her more pain, and a declaration of your commitment to her.

The order is not haphazard, either. If you want to make it past your wife's defenses, first communicate to her that you aren't attacking her, but taking responsibility for your own actions that have hurt her. Once she realizes you won't hurt her, she may listen long enough to hear you sincerely say, "I know that I've hurt you, and I'm sorry for the pain I've caused." If you then tell her your commitment to change, then she can know what you are *thinking*, how you are *feeling*, and what you plan on *doing* about your relationship with her.

Deliver all three of these messages in this order. Your wife won't care what you think about how you've hurt her if she doesn't know how badly you feel about having hurt her. And she won't care how badly you feel about hurting her if she doesn't know how you plan to stop hurting her in the future.

Remember this threefold verbal effort goes a long way toward establishing a climate in which healing can take place between you and your wife.

You may insist you've tried that before—saying, "I'm sorry and I won't do it again"—and nothing is any better now than it was before you apologized. She doesn't seem to believe you. That's why it's important to know not only *what* you should say, but to carefully consider *why* you say it. To create a climate for healing, you must communicate the right thing for the right reason.

Why We Should Say What We Say

Many men have undoubtedly tried to communicate at least some of the above messages to their wives, only to have their attempts blow up in their faces. For some, the reason their communication was not well-received was probably because the motive behind their words was selfish. They wanted to end their own pain, not commit themselves to walk with their wives through their recovery process. If they just said the magic words, everything would be better. So they gave a confession (of sorts), expressed their regret for hurting their wife, and made a commitment not to do it again.

But a wife quickly notices if a man is less interested in her than in himself. *Does he really want to be my friend,* she thinks, *or does he simply want relief from his own pain?*

We know this is what happens, for we speak to a number of women who tell us, "My husband says he's sorry and that he won't do the things that hurt me ever again. But the minute I turn around, he's back to his old ways." In frustration they throw up their hands and say, "He'll never change."

For many men, the reason behind such a disparity between their words and their behavior is that they don't fully understand what they're doing that's so painful to their wives. They don't make the connection between their wives' abusers and accomplices from the past and their own attitudes and actions in the present. They don't want to hurt their wives, but they truly don't grasp what hurts them and so they don't stop.

Other men may accurately communicate their heart, but they don't know how to follow through with their commitment to be a friend. They don't know how to act like a friend to their wives. (We will discuss several strategies for following through on verbal commitments in chapter 12—strategies that help those who are properly motivated to follow through on being a friend to their wives.)

The discrepancy between words and behavior in some

men is rooted in their motives. They may say the right things to their wives—not for their wives' good, however, but for their own. The motive makes all the difference.

To check your motives before communicating these important messages to your wife, ask yourself what you expect to happen as the result of saying the right things to your wife. If you expect things to get better immediately, you probably have your benefit more in mind than your wife's. If you expect her to meet you halfway, your motive might be to get her to change— or at least move in a direction *toward* you, rather than away from you. You don't like the current situation, so you try to manipulate it with the right words so that you get what you want.

As long as your motives are for your own gain, as good as the message may be that you communicate, it won't establish a climate in which healing takes place.

Your motives are pure if you can communicate these messages to your wife because it's the right thing to do, not for some benefit you hope to receive. You acknowledge your responsibility for doing things that hurt her because it's true. You express your sorrow for hurting her because you're sincerely sorry. You declare your commitment to be her friend because that's what you intend to do without reservation. You communicate the truth to her, knowing that the truth sets people free.

If your motives are correct, then it's no problem if your wife responds with, "I've heard that before." Her words may sting, but you remain confident that you've begun the process of reconciliation.

Having a right motive means we acknowledge that we may need to say the same thing over and over again to our wife before she can hear it and can begin to believe it. Trust is a fragile thing—easy to shatter and difficult to rebuild. But she's right. She *has* heard those promises before. The only way your wife will trust what you tell her is if you constantly repeat a consistent message, and then follow through with actions. To follow this long road to restoration requires more than selfish motivation. It requires a commitment to another person's best interest in spite of the personal cost.

In chapter 10 Sid described his turning point, when he felt convicted to make more personal sacrifices in order to be a friend to his wife during her recovery. At a time when they both could focus, he sat down with her in the living room to communicate these important messages to her.

> Honey, I'm sorry for the ways that I have been self-centered. I know that I've hurt you in many ways, and I'm really sorry. I don't want to hurt you—in fact, I want to be on your side through all of this. I want to be your friend. I intend to do several things that I think will help me to keep from hurting you further.

He then listed each specific thing.

Finally, he gave her a small ceramic butterfly with this note:

> Dear Nan, while I've been away, I've been thinking of you and praying for you. When I saw this, I knew I had to get it for you because it captures the essence of what I'm asking the Lord for on your behalf. I'm praying that in his grace and by his power he will free you from the ugliness of your past (like the caterpillar), that he will loose the bonds that hold you (like the cocoon), and that he will free you (like the butterfly). This gift represents my prayers for you and my trust in God that one day you'll be free to live in the beauty of all he has created you to be and all that is within you. I love you with all my heart. Sid.

When you find out your wife was sexually abused, don't let the words get in the way (as the song says). Instead communicate what needs to be said with the proper motive, and you will begin to establish a climate in which healing instead of further hurting can take place.

Still, words are only hot air unless they are followed by right actions. The next chapter deals with the actions that speak even more loudly than your words.

Questions for Thought and Discussion

1. How can you ensure the proper motive when you speak with your wife?

2. Have you ever tried confessing your hurtful behavior to your wife? What were the results?

3. Have you previously tried expressing your sorrow? What were the results?

4. Have you tried declaring your commitment? What were the results?

5. Why do you think it's important to include all three messages in this order when communicating terms of peace with your wife?

6. Try communicating all three messages together. Write the results here.

Chapter Twelve
Doing What Comes Unnaturally

TV's prototypical males reign for about a decade. The sixties favored Ward Cleaver of "Leave It to Beaver." Always happy and smiling, never weary after a long day at the office, he was the benevolent master of his peaceful castle. The seventies gave us a disparaging view of men: while women marched for their rights, Archie Bunker of "All in the Family" dominated his unruly row house as a coarse, opinionated bigot.

Tim "The Tool Man" Taylor of "Home Improvement" is the man's man for this decade. He aspires to wield "more power" while trying to be sensitive, but he blunders his way along, his foot more often in his mouth than on the ground. His attempts at nurturing relationships regularly move him to do something that doesn't come naturally to him—usually with disastrous results.

Learning to do what comes unnaturally is exactly what you must learn when you discover your wife was sexually abused. Your grasp of four "counterintuitive" principles in particular is necessary—"counterintuitive" because in order for a man to practice these principles, he must do the opposite of what he naturally would do in the situation.

Draw Her Near, Don't Push Her Away

It's a vivid memory for John—standing at the front door of his house after a tiring day at the office and thinking, *I really don't want to go in there and face the pain and frustration that's waiting for me.* All he wanted to do was distance himself from his wife to avoid his own personal pain.

Most men feel the same way in that situation. But if you want to be a friend to your wife during her recovery, practice the counterintuitive principle of drawing her near rather than pushing her away.

Hurting people have needs that make you want to run away, their needs are so overwhelming. We fear the intense emotions that hurting people express because we don't know how to respond to them. We are afraid of their demands because we don't know how to say no without appearing self-centered and unloving. We fear getting verbally abused in the process. Other times we push hurting people away only because we feel helpless to help them.

The fear in some men pressures them to abandon their wives. The typical man is more subtle—he silently wishes that his wife would go away, and come back only when she's recovered. He tries to hide his feeling, but what he feels, he acts on. So he pushes his wife away without realizing it. He can do this in a number of subtle ways—working late, accepting a job that requires more travel, signing up for a city-league baseball team or service organization. A desire to put distance between oneself and a hurting wife inevitably works its way out. It's a common way for men to avoid dealing with the painful intensity of their wives' emotions during recovery.

Though your natural response may be to keep your wife at arm's length or push her away, the counterintuitive response is to draw your wife near. A husband helping his wife through her recovery must be *physically present* with her. When our wives were reliving the pain of their past, the most helpful thing we could do was simply be with them. Sid can remember lingering after dinner with his wife as she felt the pain of her past. Instead of rushing off to read the paper or begin some project around the house, he dried the dishes while she washed, or sat next to her while she was reading or relaxing.

Sometimes he just held her—which can be the greatest remedy for a hurting heart. A hug says, "I care and I want to be with you." At times, though, a woman in recovery won't want you to even touch her. An innocent touch feels to her like a violation, an act of trespass, regardless of your motive. To help her past that misconception, don't let every hug be a prelude to love-making. That's not what she wants right now. Hug her because you want to show her that you care, not because you want to have sex with her.

Empathize, Don't Analyze

Being there physically with her is good, but not enough. A husband must be there emotionally for her as well. This can be tough, for men tend to be analytical by nature. From day one, a boy dismantles toys, old appliances, anything—just to discover how it works. My boys regularly ask, "Can we take it apart, Dad?" Such boys grow into men who continue to enjoy analyzing how something works, or figuring out how to make it work better. The tendency can be profitable—unless you're dealing with your wife.

The husbands I know get occasionally frustrated by trying to figure out their wives. Like trying to pick up Jell-O with a fork, they say it's often a seemingly impossible task. Figuring out a woman who is recovering from past sexual abuse is even more complicated.

When John walked into his dark apartment that autumn afternoon and found Jeanne huddled under the blankets and unable to explain her uncontrollable weeping, his first impulse was to help her analyze it. His attempt to comfort her sounded like this: "You may not know what's wrong right now, but I'm sure we can figure it out." A classic male response: analyze the problem, determine a course of action, then implement the steps leading to the solution. Not that he analyzed with selfish motives. Like most husbands, John wanted to help his wife find her way out of a very painful situation. He wasn't thinking of making his own life easier.

But your wife doesn't need your analysis—she needs your empathy. She wants your support, not your answers. If you want to help your wife during her recovery, then learn what it means to be *emotionally present* with her.

The Old Testament book of Job provides a clear picture of what it means to be emotionally present with another person. The troubles of Job are legendary: he lost his servants, his wealth, his health, his children. He was reduced to scraping his oozing sores while sitting on an ash heap outside the city limits. Three friends visited Job to comfort him in his misery—though by now they hardly recognized him, he had become so disfigured by his illness. Overwrought with grief, his friends wept and grieved and mourned over the trouble that had befallen Job.

These friends were emotionally present with Job. They connected with him at the level of the heart. Although they became discouragingly analytical before long, at least they began by communicating how sad they were that Job was in so much pain.

A husband can help his hurting wife as she goes through her recovery in the same way. As the pain of the past brings tears to her eyes and etches lines in her face, her husband can best support her not by analyzing the situation, but by letting her know how he feels about her suffering, by communicating to her how sorry he is that she's in so much pain.

People don't care how much you know until they know how much you care, says the adage. Your wife doesn't care about your analysis of her problem (even if it's a correct one). She doesn't care if you know what her next step should be out of her present darkness and toward recovery. All she hungers to know is that you care about her.

"You just don't care!" A husband in your circumstances hears this a lot. It may not be true, but your wife's perception tells you what she needs: a demonstration of your emotional care for her, in terms she can acknowledge and appreciate.

The difference between *taking care of* your wife and *caring about* your wife is the difference between analyzing and being emotionally present. Most men find it easier to take care of their wives than to care about their wives. They bring home the paychecks and make sure she gets what she needs. But it's another story convincing her that you care about her, for it requires the difficult counterintuitive principle of being emotionally present. When this principle is put into action, the analysis stops and the empathy begins.

When a man stays in his analysis mode, he only hurts his wife. The message she hears from all his analyzing is "You may not be able to figure this out, but I can." It sounds to her as if she's not as intelligent or as capable as he is; otherwise, she would have figured all of this out by now.

She doesn't need a commentary on her competency—she needs her husband to connect with her heart.

So if we're not supposed to analyze her situation, what are we to do? Empathize with her by validating her emotions. Acknowledge to her that she has every reason to feel the way she does. When she expresses anger about her abuser, verbally validate her emotions—"I'd be angry with him, too, if he did that to me." Validate her sadness—"It makes me sad to think that because of the abuse, you never had that special relationship that fathers can have with their daughters." Let her know that she has a right to feel the way she does—that if the two of you traded positions, you would feel like she does. In the midst of great confusion, your wife needs to know that you think she is right to feel as she does.

Not that you always need words to validate your wife's emotions. Job's friends cried with him. There's no reason we can't cry with our wives too, except that we've forgotten how because when we were little we heard over and over that big boys don't cry.

John remembers a particular episode of trying—again—to convince his wife that he truly loved her. At that time she was questioning the legitimacy of all her relationships, including their marriage. For several days his logical arguments and precisely worded affirmations of love merely hit the wall. They didn't come close to touching her. He was at his wits' end, defeated. One afternoon he walked into the bedroom where she was and sat on the edge of the bed.

"I know that nothing I can say can convince you that I love you. But I do love you," he told her. And then, inexplicably, with no warning, the tears began streaming down his face. It surprised both of them.

That was the moment when she began believing that he was telling the truth. So it happens that, in spite of a normal tendency to hide emotion, as we get in touch with the feelings deep inside us the emotions work their way to the surface—and in the process, work wonders in a marriage to a recovering wife.

As men we may have grown up competing with others instead of naturally showing compassion to them. Our natural response as an adult, then, is to do anything *but* connect emotionally with another person. So we end up suppressing our own emotions and ignoring the feelings of others. But the counter-intuitive response is to emotionally connect with your wife. Show her you care by validating her emotions, not by analyzing her problems.

Listen, Don't Talk

Add to a physical and emotional presence with your wife

your mental presence. Being *mentally present* means *listening* instead of talking.

Despite all of the jokes about how much women talk, men can do a pretty good job of it themselves. In fact, some men can't live without the drone of their own voices. Talking follows closely with our propensity to analyze. After all, what good is our expert analysis if we don't tell it to someone—especially our wives?

Other men may be no better at listening, but choose silence instead of speaking. These men prefer to let their wives do all the talking. But remaining quiet doesn't mean that they are listening. We can be silent and still not hear a word our wives are saying. So whether a man naturally responds to his wife by speaking or by silence, the necessary counterintuitive response is to listen.

Most women would tell you that their husbands do a fairly sloppy job of listening. Listening effectively requires a great deal of energy too, because you must intensely focus your mind on what your wife is saying. That's why we also call this counterintuitive response being *mentally* present with your wife.

The man who wants to know what to do when his wife is recovering from past sexual abuse becomes a good listener. Listening means paying close enough attention to know both what your wife says and how she feels. While it's usually easy to grasp the *content* of your wife's communication, it can be downright difficult to discern her *feelings*. Armed with the information in chapter 9 (a husband appearing to his wife as abuser or accomplice), you can begin to listen *between* her words: for instance, is she feeling abused by you? Listening to her in this manner tells you if she is feeling uncared for, neglected, or ignored, which feelings are similar to the ones the accomplices in her past brought on.

A good listener, rather than sitting in stony silence passively storing up information, provides feedback to his wife that tells her that he understands what she's saying and how she's feeling. The best way to do that is by "reflective listening"—reflecting back to her the content she has given you and the feelings you are picking up about what she is saying.

A woman recovering from past abuse was frustrated by a passive, unresponsive child. "I can't stand it when he doesn't respond to me when I tell him something," she complained.

The typical male response would be, "As I think about the situation, it seems to me that your past abuse is playing into this communication problem."

The counterintuitive response would be, "It seems you're feeling very angry over your son's passivity. That would be frustrating."

A counterintuitive response analyzes the woman's situation less and validates her feelings more. By reflecting the essence of her content, you let her know that you've been listening to her. Good listeners show they're listening by reflecting both the content and the emotions of the person to whom they are listening.

In conversations with your wife, your natural response may be to talk too much or to sit in passive silence. The necessary counterintuitive response is to listen for both *what* she says and *how* she feels. Such a response demands that we be mentally present with our wife.

Pray, Don't Preach

This is being *spiritually present* with your wife. Husbands tend to preach at their wives, to tell them what they should be doing. When she says she's tired of going to church and tired of responding to "How are you doing?" (because she isn't doing well and doesn't want to give the perfunctory "Fine!")—at that point husbands characteristically launch into a sermon about not forsaking the assembling of yourselves together. She needs to be with other people who share her faith, we exhort her.

If she's angry at her abuser, our sermon is "Forgiving Others from the Heart" (Matt. 18:35). While it may be true that she needs to forgive (as discussed in chapter 8) and that real healing and freedom come to her only to the degree that she can forgive, our preaching at her only compounds her guilt and anger.

If she's feeling uncertain that God loves her (after all, he allowed such devastating events in her past), we may unwisely try to protect God, quoting verses that speak of his love for his people. We try to persuade her that God does love her and that he must have had a good reason for not stopping her from being hurt in the past.

Of course, we never have the slightest clue why God allowed her abuse. As God said through his prophet, "'For my thoughts are not your thoughts, neither are your ways my ways,' declares the LORD. 'As the heavens are higher than the earth, so are my ways higher than your ways and my thoughts than your thoughts'" (Isa. 55:8–9). Attempting to answer the unanswerable, protecting God, safeguarding her faith—these tactics block the appropriate counterintuitive response of allowing her to keep a straight-line relationship with God. Better we should pray for her than preach at her.

During your wife's struggles, pray with her often—even when she doesn't feel like saying a prayer herself. Coming alongside her to support her before the throne of God will let her know that you are spiritually present with her, yet without giving the impression that you are trying to be God's spokesman. At some point the husband of a wife who is in recovery from past sexual abuse must learn that he will not be the one who brings healing to his wife—the Lord is her healer. A husband can go to great lengths to create a climate in which restoration may occur, but God restores wholeness.

Sid vividly remembers when Nancy was visited by God, who brought her a new measure of healing. She couldn't understand how God could love her in light of how dirty she felt because of having been abused. Late one night after she and Sid talked and prayed and read Scripture together, the Lord flooded her with the assurance that he loved her unconditionally—regardless of how she felt about what had taken place in her past. He gave her an image of herself, clothed in white garments. And she heard him say, "You are clean before me."

Being spiritually present is a method of waging spiritual warfare on our wife's behalf through prayer against an enemy, the Devil, who is called in the Bible the "accuser of the brethren." One of the Devil's tactics is to defeat people by fueling their guilt. Battling a spiritual enemy such as this can only be done with spiritual weapons, and the most effective weapon is not a sermon, but a prayer.

Though your natural response may be to preach at your wife in an attempt to align her with the faith you hold dear, the counterintuitive response is to be spiritually present with her through prayer.

Maybe you've noticed something about these counterintuitive principles—that if we do just the opposite of what we are naturally inclined to do, then we're often on the right track. Instead of pushing her away, we draw her near. Instead of analyzing her problem, we empathize with her by validating her emotions. Instead of talking at her, we listen to her. Instead of preaching at her, we pray for her.

These are the actions that demonstrate you are her friend. These actions create the climate in which the Lord can work to bring wholeness to your wife beyond your expectations.

Questions for Thought and Discussion

1. Which of the counterintuitive principles do you most need to put into practice?

2. How will your practice of this principle help your wife in her recovery?

3. Who will help you stay accountable to learning this new way of relating to your wife?

4. When will you start putting these principles into practice?

Conclusion:
The Incredible Journey

Although recovery from past sexual abuse has a discernible beginning point, it's a process, not an event. For that reason its conclusion—the point at which the process of recovery is over—can't be nearly so well-defined as its start.

To conclude our efforts with this book, however, let's review where we've been. First, our purpose in writing is to support men who experience the secondary effects of past sexual abuse during their wife's recovery. We hope that the sharing of our experiences, as well as those of other men, helps you to realize that you are not alone. Many men have faced the same struggles you are facing, they have felt the same emotions you are feeling, and they have asked the same questions you are asking.

Second, we attempted to give you some insight into the choices available to you, into what support you need to get from a friend, and into the process your wife is going through and your role in that process. We wanted you to see how easily a husband can enter into the role of an abuser or an accomplice without even realizing it. Yet we assured you that it's worth the price to learn to be your wife's friend.

Finally, we discussed ways you can not only survive the turmoil, but can also play a significant part in your wife's recovery. By communicating more constructive messages in appropriate ways and by practicing the counterintuitive principles, you can begin to foster the kind of relationship that you have always wanted with your wife.

You begin by taking a first step. Put into practice one principle or one insight you have gained. As your wife is in a process of recovery, you, too, are in a process—learning how to relate in new and different ways to the person she is becoming. Your incredible journey will be painful, but we encourage you to persevere. You have nothing to lose and everything to gain, both personally and in your relationship with your wife. The reward of personal growth that results from your efforts is a treasure you will cherish for a lifetime.

Appendix A

Commonly Asked Questions and Answers

Q. What role does the therapist play in my wife's recovery?

A. The therapist-client relationship is a contract of sorts, with obligations on both sides. The client commits to pay the agreed-upon fee, to show up for her regularly scheduled sessions, and to work toward mutually set goals. The therapist commits to be available to the client and to help the client establish and work toward constructive goals that result in personal growth. Since no two people are identical, the role the therapist plays is dynamic and constantly changing, allowing for only a few generalizations.

Modeling healthy relationships to their clients is one of the primary roles of a therapist or counselor. Healthy relationships are characterized by trust, honest and open communication, and mutuality. Let's look at each of these characteristics of a healthy relationship in more detail, briefly highlighting the role of the therapist in each case. Keep in mind that the therapist may be cast in multiple roles concurrently and the dominant role may change during the course of therapy.

- *Trust.* The therapist often earns the client's trust through consistent expressions of love, compassion, and acceptance. Ideally, parents play this role in the lives of their children resulting in a strong, healthy sense of security and self-worth for the child. For many women recovering from past sexual abuse, who grew up with parents who failed to provide these desperately needed expressions of love, the therapist becomes a *pseudo-parent*. The therapist provides the love and acceptance that the client never received as a child, and helps the client to work toward freedom from insecurity and toward a more accurate self-image. This often lengthy process may never completely compensate for the lack of parental love during the client's childhood.

- *Honest and open communication.* By fostering a secure environment, where truth is prized and courageously sought, the therapist helps the client learn the value of honest and open communication in a relationship. The therapist helps the client face the truth about herself and others. With no hidden agendas or false loyalties, the therapist is ideally interested only in the client's welfare. In the therapy session, no topic is off-limits. Everything can and should be discussed openly, without shame or fear of judgment.

As someone who is "unshockable" or who "has heard it all before," the therapist provides a secure setting within which clients can reveal their innermost thoughts, fears, or painful memories. By taking the client seriously and not minimizing her pain or ignoring significant facts, the therapist promotes the client's growth through legitimate suffering. In his book *The Road Less Traveled*, Dr. M. Scott Peck eloquently describes the need for suffering in the healing process.

> Fearing the pain involved, almost all of us, to a greater or lesser degree, attempt to avoid problems. . . . We attempt to get out of them rather than suffer through them. This tendency to avoid problems and the emotional suffering inherent in them is the primary basis of all human mental illness. . . . When we avoid the legitimate suffering that results

> from dealing with problems, we also avoid the growth that problems demand from us. It is for this reason that in chronic mental illness we stop growing, we become stuck. And without healing, the human spirit begins to shrivel.[1]

The therapist promotes the client's search for truth by providing an honest assessment of reality and creating a context for legitimate suffering in a supportive setting.

- *Mutuality.* The therapist promotes a sense of commitment and mutuality by providing the client with insight, encouragement, and respect. The therapist is a true partner with the client, helping the client to understand the characteristics of normal, healthy behavior in relationships. To the woman in recovery from past sexual abuse, the therapist offers insight into the abuse and into new ways of understanding herself and others. The therapist also provides encouragement during times of great suffering for the client, promoting the necessary healing while allowing the client to grow at her own pace.

The therapist also assists the client to develop respect for herself and others and to create a strong sense of personal identity. The therapist's assistance involves setting appropriate limits with respect to the client and fostering a sense of personal responsibility. The therapist may set an expectation regarding the client's commitment to show up for her regularly scheduled sessions, for example, by saying, "I understand that on occasion you will be unable to make it to our sessions due to your job requirements. But unless you give me twenty-four hours advance notice that you will be unable to attend, I will still charge you for the session. I have set aside that time each week just for you, and I will be here, ready to meet with you. I expect you to be here unless I hear from you otherwise." While this particular interaction may be difficult for the client, the therapist effectively models the mutual respect and commitment that characterize healthy relationships.

Obviously, the complex role of the therapist cannot be adequately described in a few paragraphs, and the preceding explanation provides a simplified and somewhat idealized view. In addition, numerous models of therapy and diverse modes of treatment exist, which differ significantly from the above description that have not been addressed.

Q. **What if my wife's abuser is a family member? How should I respond to him?**

A. One of the most difficult things about your new situation is that you may know the person or persons who abused your wife, especially if the abuser is a member of her family. You may be expected to see, and even interact with, this person in social settings. You may be expected to buy gifts for him at Christmas. You may be expected to go to birthday parties for him. How do you respond to this person?

First, admit that, very understandably, you may feel anger and resentment toward this person. Your feelings are legitimate and must be validated before you can assist your wife. Either a supportive or a skilled friend can provide an avenue through which you can constructively express your feelings.

Second, acknowledge that your wife's recovery process takes priority when you consider how to respond to your wife's abuser or abusers. Avoid making her situation more difficult. When you explode in rage over the injustice done to your wife, it subtly pressures her to feel your intense feelings and distracts her from experiencing her own feelings—which may be focused differently than yours. If you share your emotions with her, be sure you express *your own* emotions and feelings rather than the anger, resentment, and bitterness you feel on your wife's behalf. In other words, don't play protector. Usually if a husband expresses his feelings of indignation and anger to a supportive or skilled friend, he can more easily avoid interjecting himself into the situation as his wife's protector. Managing his responses with a friend allows his wife to experience her own feelings and to constructively resolve her own fear and rage. Experience your own feelings, and allow her to do the same.

Third, take your cue about how to interact with the abuser from your wife—don't let your personal responses get ahead of her. It may be difficult or impossible for you to confront the person yourself, without making the situation much more complex and difficult for your wife. Although you and your feelings are important, *it is her recovery process that must be paramount during this time.* She suffered the greater injury, and her recovery takes precedence. If your wife successfully works through her own issues and feelings during the recovery process and reaches some resolution with the offending family member or members, then hopefully you can take your lead from her and reach a similar point of resolution.

Fourth, don't hold on to your resentment toward the abuser. When a woman has resolved her own feelings toward the offending family member and has moved in the direction of forgiveness, it's extremely counterproductive for her husband to maintain a vengeful and embittered attitude. Future interactions with that family member will continue to be strained, making it difficult for all concerned. In the same way that your wife owes it to herself to constructively resolve her own feelings in this matter, you must free yourself of anger and bitterness towards this person.

Keep in mind that *there can be forgiveness without restoration of the original relationship.* In other words, while both you and your wife may reach a satisfactory resolution regarding the past abuse, the relationship with this family member may never be fully restored to its original state of trust and respect. Things will never be the same with this person. Ideally, the husband can resolve his own feelings in this matter and can work through them at the same time his wife is processing her feelings, without negatively affecting her recovery process.

Although an enormous challenge for most husbands, pacing the processing of your own feelings to your wife's recovery is an important ingredient in being supportive of her. It also encourages you to take seriously your responsibility to deal constructively with your own feelings of anger, resentment, and bitterness. These feelings, if fully embraced over a long period of time, extract a high toll from you. Allow yourself to be free of them and to get on with your life, rather than holding onto these feelings indefinitely and suffering the long-term negative consequences of doing so.

Last, discuss your situation briefly with your wife, without expressing all of your feelings of anger and bitterness toward the offending family member or members. Explain that you are processing your own feelings of anger towards the family member with the help of a supportive or skilled friend. Assure her that you don't want your process to negatively impact what she is going through and that you are trying to be supportive of her by responding in this way.

Once you have communicated your plan to your wife, chances are good that she will appreciate both your honesty and support and your intention to allow her the freedom to express and work through her own feelings without inappropriately interjecting yourself into the process as her protector. Discussing the issue in this manner also reinforces your role as her ally—you are on her side and are treating her with respect as someone who is capable of working through her own recovery.

Working through the practical issues raised when a family member is responsible for your wife's abuse poses difficult questions with no pat answers. Each situation is unique, and any action should be carefully considered in the light of your fundamental goal to be supportive of your wife's recovery process while recognizing and legitimizing your own feelings and working through them.

Q. Why does my wife insist that "my issues" are what's causing so many problems in our relationship? We were doing fine until now, and I haven't changed.

A. Inevitably, the significant changing of one person in a marriage unbalances the relationship. Keeping in mind that people are attracted to one another for a reason, it's likely that each of you has weaknesses for which you each must compensate. Although it is advantageous when one person's strength complements the other's weakness, the same dynamic can occur destructively within the relationship—one person's dysfunctional thought patterns or behaviors are complemented by their spouse's dysfunctional thought patterns or behaviors.

Spouses rarely deliberately interact in unhealthy ways. Rather your unconcious choices of dysfunctional behavior balance each other out. That's why it appeared that things were "doing fine" as long as no one changed. What your wife means by "your issues" is those areas of interaction between you that are unhealthy, but have been pervasive in the relationship, and in which she no longer wants to participate. Often, as a result of her recovery process, she begins to see ways in which the two of you have interacted that are destructive, either to the relationship or to her personally. Obviously, she wants these interactions to change and is strong enough (maybe for the first time) to confront you about them.

Your wife's readiness to confront you means that you need to hear what she is saying and carefully consider what you are going to do about it. *Chances are that you too, will need to change.* Only in this way will things get back into balance—a healthy balance this time.

Q. **How can I best respond to the often repeated question of "Where's your wife?"**

A. When your wife begins her recovery from past sexual abuse, she may withdraw from people. Having been terribly hurt by other people during the time of her abuse, she may fear being open and vulnerable or trusting in others lest she be hurt again. This is especially true as she relives the events of her abusive past and experiences the fear and rage associated with those painful days.

As her husband, you are one of the people she may also withdraw from. You need to understand what is taking place and not perceive her withdrawal as a personal rejection, but take it for what it is—part of the process necessary for her healing to take place. Frankly, she may not have the emotional or physical strength to deal with the interpersonal conflicts and tensions that are present in most relationships, because the battle with her past is so overwhelming. Rather than expending energy she doesn't have in trying to maintain her relationships with others, it may be easier for your wife to withdraw until she feels like she has the strength to re-engage in those relationships. You may come to understand this, but what about others? When you show up at social functions or at church by yourself, you will hear the same questions over and over again, including, "Where is your wife?" or a common variant of that question, "Is your wife sick?"

The more your wife withdraws from her relationships, the more people are likely to question you about her well-being and the more uncomfortable you will probably become. You may feel as though people are holding you personally responsible for your wife's not being in attendance. If so, you may begin to resent her for this, or feel irritated with them. You may also feel caught between telling them the truth about what your wife is going through and protecting her privacy. Understandably, it is a difficult situation for most husbands to deal with in a constructive manner.

Perhaps one good approach is to sit down with your wife and tell her of your discomfort at not knowing exactly what to say in response to people who ask you where she is or how she is doing. Together you may be able to craft a response that is acceptable to both of you; a response that is truthful and at the same time is sensitive to her situation and to your needs. You may decide to give people who have a close relationship with your wife more information than her casual acquaintances, but the bottom line is that she should be the one to decide who needs to know what. If possible, it will probably be helpful for her to communicate directly with her closest friends because they may feel the same rejection that you felt as she withdraws from them. Her personal contact with them will probably help them to understand better the changes that are taking place in her life and in their relationship with her.

Q. What do you say to the kids?

A. One of the questions we are often asked is, "What do you say and do for your children in the midst of this crisis?" It is an excellent question, since your children will be experiencing the same changing situation as you and may feel some of the same feelings you are, but without the same level of understanding. In this case, we encourage men to try to be sensitive to both their children and their wives.

To make your wife out to be the "bad guy" during this time or to imply that something is wrong with her is neither accurate nor productive. At the same time it is not helpful to your children for you to just pretend that nothing is happening and hope that they simply ignore the evidence that they can plainly see of the difficulty the family is experiencing. We have three suggestions for husbands in this situation. First, try to encourage your children to talk about their feelings. This will help keep them from internalizing all of their emotions and will help you to identify specific areas of difficulty that they might be having. Second, try to help them understand, as best they can, what their mother is going through, without mentioning the abuse itself, to help alleviate any false guilt that they may be experiencing. This explanation will vary greatly depending on the ages of your children. Third, when they do something that "pushes a button" and provokes an immediate negative reaction, try to help them learn what they can do to help avoid similar situations in the future.

I remember occasions when Nancy would get angry with our son over something that he had said or done, only to later realize that she had overreacted because he had pushed a button related to her past abuse. I know that she felt terrible about what had happened and would always make it a point to ask his forgiveness and try to help him understand what was happening. I also made a deliberate effort to take him aside after an incident to ask him how he was feeling. After listening to him, I would simply explain to him that Mom wasn't feeling very well in terms he could understand and I would try to help him realize that from time to time we all treat others in ways that they don't like and may not deserve. Then I would try to give him some practical ideas about how he could do things differently in the future to be more sensitive to his mother during this time.

If you think about it, our answer to this question is similar in many respects to our response to the question this entire book attempts to answer, "What do you do when you find out your wife was sexually abused?" We began by trying to help you get in touch with some of the feelings you might be feeling when confronted by this crisis. We then tried to help you understand what your wife is going through.

Finally, we tried to give you some insights into how to live with your wife during this time in a way that is sensitive to the difficult process she is experiencing. You can take many of the principles we have talked about in this book and use them to help your children process the changes that are taking place in their lives as their mother recovers from her past abuse.

Q. I've heard that women who have been victims of past sexual abuse tend to marry men who have been victims as well. Is this true?

A. While it has been suggested that victims of past sexual or physical abuse tend to marry one another, it has been postulated as equally likely that victims of past sexual abuse tend to marry actual or potential abusers. Still others claim that there is no relationship between these factors. The authors are unaware of any research which has been done to actually measure whether or not any of these claims are statistically valid. Based on our contact with hundreds of men in our seminars, most of whose wives have suffered past sexual abuse, we have encountered some men who have been abused, and some who have admitted to being past abusers. Throughout, we have not noticed a discernible pattern. It is important to note, however, that as absurd as it may sound, *people are attracted to one another for a reason.*

In fact, people are attracted to others for many different reasons. These attractions are always influenced by the important experiences and relationships that we had growing up, including any experience of abuse. However, this can point a person in any one or more of several different directions. Possibly they are attracted to someone who is gentle and affectionate or someone who is good at caring for others. Perhaps it is something else about a person that they find compelling. But often these attractions to another person may have their roots in an abusive and painful past.

Q. What if the woman in my life who has been sexually abused is not my wife? Can I still be of help to her and involved in her recovery process?

A. You may know of a close friend or loved one who has suffered past sexual abuse and is in the process of recovery. It is only natural to want to help and support those people that we care about, but is it always appropriate or helpful? Many of the dynamics that we have talked about in the book seem to be particular to husbands and wives. This is due to the fact that living with someone and interacting with them on a daily basis over a period of years tends to bring out certain emotions, feelings, and interactions that might not otherwise be present in the relationship. Since you are not this person's spouse, you cannot expect to necessarily have a central role in her recovery process. But depending on the person involved and your level of closeness with her, you may indeed be able to provide significant support. (Many of the following suggestions apply equally well to men who are in the process of recovery from past abuse.)

   Due to the intensity of the recovery process, it is likely that a woman going through this process will not interact on a deep emotional level with very many people, but instead will try and surround herself with a few key individuals who will provide her with understanding and support. If you are not one of these key individuals, then probably the best way for you to help is to pray for her. This kind of support is discussed in more detail in the final paragraph.

   If you happen to have a very close relationship with the woman who is in recovery, but she is not your wife, then you might want to provide support in one of the following ways. Assuming that she is aware that you have knowledge of the abuse and is not reluctant to talk about it with you, you might make yourself available to her to be one of her supportive friends during this time. You can tell her that you are available to simply listen to how she is feeling and to provide general emotional support during a very draining and exhausting process. By being one of the people who is available to her and providing her an opportunity to talk about her past, you are also helping to break the accomplice-like role of secrecy, where people know about the past abuse, but the subject is taboo. By allowing her to talk freely about her recovery, you break those bonds of secrecy and provide important support as well.

There may be other practical things that you can do for her. Perhaps you can pick the kids up after practice or make a meal for her or her family. Just offering to be available to make her life a little easier during that time can be of invaluable help and support. There are certainly other things that may be of help, but these are a few of the ways that you can provide love and support for a woman in recovery, even if she is not your wife.

For you men who might know of a woman who is a friend and is in recovery, clearly good judgment should be used in terms of trying to provide emotional support for her during this time. It can be a time of great emotional upheaval and confusion and you certainly don't want to add to that turmoil through any inappropriate actions on your part.

Regardless of any other role that you may have in the life of a woman recovering from past sexual abuse, one powerful thing that you can do for her is to pray for her. We are not suggesting that you pray that her recovery process would be free of pain, but that she would know the comfort of God and close friends during this time, and that she would emerge from this painful process with more strength, clarity, and confidence than she has ever known before.

Notes

Introduction

1. Rich Buhler, *Pain and Pretending* (Nashville: Thomas Nelson, 1991), 32–33. Another good resource for those looking for information on sexual abuse is Dan Allender's *The Wounded Heart* (Colorado Springs: NavPress, 1992).
2. Ibid., 32.
3. *Los Angeles Times,* 25 August 1985.

Chapter 1

1. Rich Buhler, *Pain and Pretending* (Nashville: Thomas Nelson, 1991), 31.
2. Clifford and Joyce Penner, *A Gift For All Ages* (Waco: Word, 1986), 224.

Chapter 6

1. Gary Richmond, *The Divorce Decision* (Waco: Word, 1988), 12.
2. Henry Cloud, *Changes That Heal* (Grand Rapids: Zondervan, 1992), 92.
3. Henry Cloud and John Townsend, *Boundaries* (Grand Rapids: Zondervan, 1992), 151.

Chapter 7

1. Ken Druck, *The Secrets Men Keep*, (Garden City, N.Y.: Doubleday, 1985), 23.
2. James Wagenvoord, ed., *Men: A Book for Women* (New York: Avon Books, 1978), 165.

Chapter 8

1. While other representations of the recovery process may be equally valid, we created this model to facilitate understanding of the primary stages of

recovery. We avoided using technical jargon, choosing instead words that can easily be remembered.

2. David G. Benner, *Healing Emotional Wounds* (Grand Rapids: Baker, 1990), 53–57.

3. Ibid., 56.

4. It is understood that Jesus is talking primarily about his Word in this text; it highlights the fact that those who know what he says will be set free, but the principle applies to all of life. The truth sets us free from the bondage of deception.

5. Benner, *Healing Emotional Wounds*, 108.

6. M. Scott Peck, *Further Along the Road Less Traveled* (New York: Simon and Schuster, 1993), 87–88.

Questions and Answers

1. M. Scott Peck, *The Road Less Traveled* (New York: Simon and Schuster, 1978), 16–17.

For more information regarding materials, tapes, seminars, or speaking engagements, write:

Dr. Sid Rogers or John Courtright
12627 S. Santa Gertrudes Ave., Suite A
La Mirada, California 90638